of
Vice
Control

Prentice-Hall
Essentials of Law Enforcement Series

James D. Stinchcomb
Series Editor

DEFENSE AND CONTROL TACTICS
George Sylvain

ELEMENTS OF CRIMINAL INVESTIGATION
Paul B. Weston and Kenneth M. Wells

HANDBOOK OF COURTROOM DEMEANOR
AND TESTIMONY
C. Alex Panteleoni

HANDBOOK OF VICE CONTROL
Denny F. Pace

PATROL OPERATIONS
Paul M. Whisenand and James L. Cline

POLICE-COMMUNITY RELATIONS
Edward Eldefonso, Alan Coffey,
and Walter Hartinger

Handbook of Vice Control

DENNY F. PACE

Program Coordinator
Police Services
Texas Criminal Justice Council

PRENTICE-HALL, INC.
Englewood Cliffs, New Jersey

HV8067
P3

© 1971 by PRENTICE-HALL, INC.
Englewood Cliffs, New Jersey

All rights reserved. No part of this book may
be reproduced in any form or by any means
without permission in writing from the publisher.

INDIANA
UNIVERSITY
D. G. T. S.
FORT WAYNE

P 13–382754–2
C 13–382762–3
Library of Congress Catalog Card Number: 70–140765
Printed in the United States of America

Current printing (last digit):
10   9   8   7   6   5   4   3   2   1

PRENTICE-HALL INTERNATIONAL, INC., London
PRENTICE-HALL OF AUSTRALIA PTY. LTD., Sydney
PRENTICE-HALL OF CANADA LTD., Toronto
PRENTICE-HALL OF INDIA PRIVATE LIMITED, New Delhi
PRENTICE-HALL OF JAPAN, INC., Tokyo

Introduction

Surely nothing can be more fundamental to guaranteeing the delivery of professional services than the employment of properly trained personnel. In pursuit of that goal, law enforcement officers and those who train them have long recognized the need for concise yet thoroughly documented information, well-researched and accurately presented.

In recent years, several commendable efforts have resulted in the availability of some valuable training resources. But too few of these were professionally developed by the textbook publishing companies, although their assistance was becoming imperative. The Prentice-Hall Essentials of Law Enforcement Series has been developed following a conference of national authorities who were asked to determine topics for priority production. The subject areas chosen are both timely and critical to the police and to their own increased determination to improve their service.

The potential use for this series is limited only by the creative imaginations of those responsible for peace officers' access to learning. Each book may perform as a supplement to a college course, as a resource for a training program, or as a reader to encourage informal study. It is the hope and the intent of the publisher, the editor, and the authors that these practical texts will contribute to the continuing progress being achieved by the nation's police.

James D. Stinchcomb

Institute for Justice
and Law Enforcement
Washington, D.C.

Preface

In the application of the various law enforcement functions, none become quite so embroiled in controversy as vice activities. As efficient police officers enforce vice laws they interpret cultural and social values through their punitive enforcement; thus, although these suppressive activities are based upon law, their applications are tempered to meet the needs of social or political factors.

Because of the social role the police acts against vice assume, it is important that concise work standards and procedures are developed for field officers involved in the enforcement of vice statutes. In addition, the community should be cognizant of police departmental organization and interaction.

The enforcement of statutes dealing with vice has been the subject of much criticism by the public. Many police officers, aware of this criticism, know that mere punitive enforcement is not the final answer for the elimination of vice crimes. A police agency does not purport to be totally effective in vice control. The best that may be expected of law enforcement is stop-gap repression until more enlightened preventive and rehabilitation methods are put into practice. Although some policemen may disagree, it is not the prerogative of the law enforcement officer to make individual decisions condoning vice violations. *Because if a given act is a violation of a statute, the enforcement officer is required to take some positive action against the violator.*

The organization of this handbook is based upon a brief discussion of social and political problems associated with vice, examples of some laws that are applicable, and a limited number of general procedures used in enforcing vice laws.

The handbook has been divided into seven chapters: (1) problems related to vice enforcement in the community;

(2) organization and internal communication for vice enforcement; (3) the legal system and vice control; (4) guidelines for the enforcement officer and specialized crimes, including (5) organized crime; (6) gambling; and (7) sex-related offenses.

This handbook presents only a general approach to vice enforcement. Each state and each city will have its unique laws and procedural problems. What may be the best procedure for the metropolitan-urban areas may not apply to rural areas. Thus, an officer in using these guidelines must take into consideration the jurisdictional policies and departmental procedures that will affect his particular agency.

Denny F. Pace

Contents

Contents

x

Handbook
of
Vice
Control

In this chapter social and political issues are raised in order to assist the field officer in gaining a broader view of community problems in the areas of vice law enforcement. These include: (1) the definition of vice; (2) general assumptions held about vice in the community; and (3) a brief observation of the political influences present in the community in which the officer must operate.

Definition of Vice

Vice is defined as a moral failing, evil or wicked conduct, corruption and depravity.[1] This definition of vice includes two different and distinct classifications of crime, which are described as *malum en se* and *malum prohibitum*. These classifications are strong indicators of the types of crimes the community will tolerate.

> *Malum en se*: A wrong in itself; and act or case involving illegality from the very nature of the transaction (e.g., rape, incest, etc.). By their very nature, crimes of this type are repugnant to a community. Strong community demands for rigid enforcement of these violations will be common.
>
> *Malum Prohibitum*: A wrong prohibited; a thing which is wrong because it is prohibited (e.g., gambling, liquor law violations, etc.). These violations will find much community support through active participation of persons who do not feel that these crimes are wrong. The very nature

[1] Webster's *New World Dictionary*, College Edition, The World Publishing Company.

chapter

1

of this type of vice makes the enforcement of such statutes difficult. Skolnick points this out by saying:

... Given the task of enforcing "unenforceable laws" it is not surprising to find police demanding working conditions from the court to lighten their burden, and if, as is presently the trend, heavier restrictions are placed upon the police, they may well ignore these or grow even more hostile toward due process principles in their attempt to enforce legal morality. Such observations demonstrate some of the difficulties created for the police as a working organization by the attempt to achieve moral consensus in a heterogeneous society through criminal punishment.[2]

Throughout this handbook there are indications that vice laws are ambiguous, inadequate, and frequently unwanted. The police officer must accept the fact that all vice violators will not be apprehended. Even so, those violators who are arrested must be apprehended through legal means. Weakness of the law does not justify illegal actions by the enforcement officer.

Some General Assumptions about Vice and General Enforcement Principles

An officer should be aware of the following assumptions:

Profit motive is the prime cause of vice activity.
　　The annual income from illegal gambling alone is estimated to be $20 to $50 billion per year.
All violations, whether committed by commercial interests or individuals, should be treated equally. The field officer should not have to interpret the difference between commercial and individual criminal activity.
The police officer should not sanction special privileges outside the law for the benefit of any community group.
Methods used in apprehension of vice violators need not be

---

[2]Jerome H. Skolnick, *Justice Without Trial* (New York: John Wiley and Sons, Inc., 1966), p. 227.

Enforcement of Vice Laws in the Community

controversial if proper policies and procedures are followed.

Electronic surveillance, for example, need not be avoided as a legitimate investigative device.

The police operator and informant, if properly instructed and supervised, need not bring discredit to a legitimate investigation.

The enforcement of vice crimes will tend to bring criticism from many sources in the community. If, however, policies regarding vice control are precise and the officer is trained, the criticism may then be directed to the law itself rather than to the enforcement agency.

Vice is the cause of many related crimes.

Embezzlement and theft are common crimes that result from vice activity.

Murder and assaults are frequent by-products of the vice activities of a city.

Vice is the profit-making enterprise of organized crime.

Vice is allowed to exist because there is little hostile public sentiment toward most forms of vice behavior; thus, there is little general public pressure to eliminate vice conditions.

In order to exist on a large scale, vice offenses require some collusion from the local governments and the community in general.

Unlike the case with other crimes, with vice crimes there are usually no complaining victims and few voluntary witnesses; thus, the necessity to enforce vice statutes becomes one of the judgment of the enforcement officer.

Contrary to popular opinion, vice activities are generally not conducted by a single person. Third-party profits are common in vice crimes.[3]

The vice officer will usually obtain information, then develop his case based upon independent facts. Because of this dependence upon received information, successful prosecutions are difficult to obtain.

The real delivery of enforcement services cannot come from the federal government. The national government may protect and assist but it does not have the capability to

[3]International City Managers' Association, *Municipal Police Administration*, 6th ed. (Chicago: I.C.M.A., 1969), p. 196.

General Assumptions about Vice and General Enforcement Principles

produce adequate enforcement and feedback to replace local enforcement agencies.

Community Influences in Vice Law Enforcement

An organization will be effective when there is a balance between the internal and external influences. The influence of political pressure groups is an important source of informal controls for the citizen. These groups assist in establishing norms and ideals.

Political Influences

An officer should be aware that:

The nature of the democratic political processes contributes to a laissez-faire program of vice enforcement. Many communities, for political and other reasons, do not like to stress vice enforcement.

The intent of the party in power, with respect to vice enforcement, may be shown through budgetary allocation and imposed restrictions on the policies of a department. The political party in power, through personnel appointments, promotional examinations, and other subtle means, can influence the degree of enforcement a community receives.

Political manipulators may use these techniques for placing law officers in the middle on controversial actions (e.g., selective enforcement such as a strong emphasis upon one type of crime while another goes unenforced and the assignment of certain types of vice cases to a given court).

Merely because civic leaders wish to maintain a closed city does not mean that existing vice conditions will disappear. Vice influences that are deeply entrenched in a community rarely yield to short-term clean-up campaigns.

Ethnic group relations are highly susceptible to vice control activities. A group that sees vice laws flaunted through organized corruptions does not attach a strong sense of wrongness to moral laws.

Enforcement of Vice Laws in the Community

Other Community Influences

In addition to political groups there are other informal groups that play important roles in the degree of enforcement expected of the police. These groups are:

> The Press
> Ethnic Groups
> Labor Unions
> Churches
> Special Interest Groups

Based upon the assumption that community groups are going to be influential in proscribing broad enforcement policies, it appears that, in vice enforcement, it is equally as important for the police officer to know *why* certain laws are enforced as it is for him to know *how* they are enforced.

In Chapter 2 organizational and communications systems are presented. They are basic to an officer's understanding as to *why* certain procedures are best in vice enforcement.

Community Influences in Vice Law Enforcement

Organization
and
Internal
Communications
for
Vice
Law
Enforcement

The manner in which a department is organized will influence the way in which vice laws are enforced. If there is a sound organizational structure and an efficient information network, vice enforcement will become a cooperative rather than an individual effort for all department personnel.

Organization

The following examples indicate some of the more common organizational structures being used by departments throughout the United States.

In small departments officers enforcing vice laws report both orally and in writing to the chief (see Fig. 2–1).

In a large department with centralized control, vice enforcement personnel report directly to the chief. In this

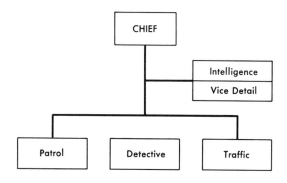

Fig. 2–1. Small centralized vice organization.

chapter

2

page 6

system there is no overlapping of unit jurisdiction (see Fig. 2–2).

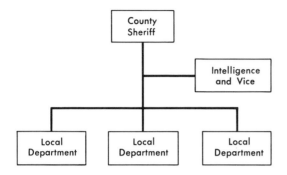

Fig. 2–2. Large centralized vice organization.

In the large decentralized department the chief delegates enforcement responsibility to bureau and precinct commanders. Information of a vice nature is transmitted through channels to the chief. Several overlapping units operate closely under the chief in the Administrative Bureau. Each unit serves as a check upon the other (see Fig. 2–3).

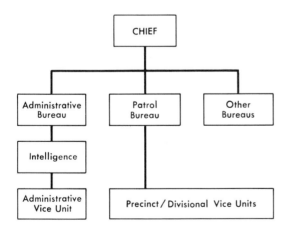

Fig. 2–3. Large decentralized vice organization.

In a cooperative county system, the local agencies furnish personnel on a rotating basis. The sheriff normally

Organization

maintains staff for the records and communications system. This type of cooperative organization is advised by a committee of representatives from each agency (see Fig. 2–4).

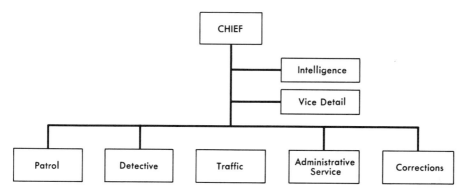

Fig. 2–4. Centralized county system consolidating forces for local agencies.

Such systems of organizational control are established to protect the department's integrity and to assure the officer that his efforts will be protected by adequate staff planning and internal supervision.

Vice Information and Records System

Vice information comes from several sources. How that information is obtained and how it is handled will be strong indicators of a department's effectiveness. The areas discussed are: (1) The basic intelligence process and information needed; (2) methods of collecting information; and (3) how a records system should function.

The Basic Intelligence Processes and Information Needed

The information needed for vice law enforcement will come from both field officer reports and the departmental

Organization and Internal Communications for Enforcement

intelligence functions. The basic field reporting function is established in the regular records system. In most departments the development of vice information through intelligence reporting has yet to be developed. Only by understanding the scope of organized crime will an officer appreciate the value of vice enforcement.

In a Dade County, Florida, study some of the following suggestions were offered as possible guides in developing procedures for the retention of information on organized crime.[1]

> Ascertaining and establishing within the police jurisdiction the extent of the existence of organized crime, its strength, organizational structure, and sources of income.
>
> Identifying current and emerging criminal leaders and their associates.
>
> Identifying areas or industries (legal or illegal) most vulnerable to organized crime.
>
> Expanding the information-gathering system to include analysis and dissemination of information back to concerned field officers.
>
> Utilizing intelligence information for determining priorities and deploying personnel in order to reflect the crime control climate of the jurisdiction.

This report divides intelligence information into two categories: tactical and strategic.

Tactical Intelligence. Most police officers are better able to identify with this type of information, which lends itself to the primary thrust of arrest and prosecution. Tactical intelligence includes:

> Information which is evidence of offenses, either substantive or of a conspiracy.
>
> Information helpful in criminal prosecutions.
>
> Information helpful in identifying active criminals.
>
> Information helpful in covering specific areas of criminal activity (geographical or by crime category).

[1] Ralph F. Salerno, *A Report for the Department of Public Safety* (Dade County, Florida, 1968), pp. 4–5. For comprehensive insight into mob activities, you are referred to Ralph Salerno and John S. Tompkins, *The Crime Confederation* (Garden City, N.Y.: Doubleday and Company, Inc., 1969).

Information helpful in identifying modus operandi and criminal associations.

Strategic Intelligence. It may be assumed that the real value of strategic intelligence is most often overlooked and underestimated and that it is not, therefore, properly utilized by police officers. This type of information may not lend itself readily to an arrest or prosecution but, nevertheless, has great value. Some uses of this information are:

> For public education in the *prevention* of certain forms of crime.
> For obtaining legislation which would be helpful in combating crime.
> In identifying target areas of police concern.
> In contributing to other decisions of government which are not directly connected to arrest and/or prosecution.
> Contributing to decisions concerning police training and curriculum.
> Obtaining the benefits of work performed by professionals in other disciplines, particularly from the academic field.

In addition, the report identifies critical areas of the county in which intelligence gathering is particularly critical. These areas are:[2]

> Waterfront
> Airports
> Labor Racketeering

These areas could, in most geographical locations, be expanded to include:

> Business areas that are subject to pressure from syndicates, such as bars, vending machines, loan operations, laundries, and others.
> Miscellaneous areas such as race tracks, sporting events, and conventions.

The national scope of the organized criminal enterprise is shown in Figure 2–5. Where these organized elements exist, there will also be vice problems.

[2]Salerno, *Report, ibid.,* p. 9.

Organization and Internal Communications for Enforcement

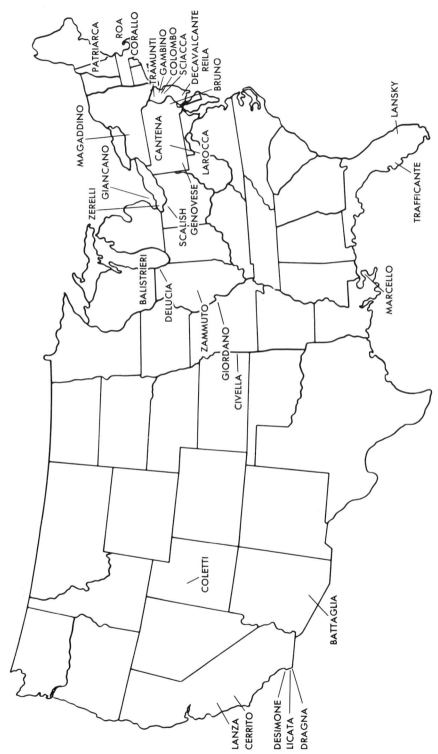

Fig. 2–5. Identified Mafia leaders and associates in the United States.

LANZA
CERRITO
DESIMONE
LICATA
DRAGNA

BATTAGLIA

COLETTI

CIVELLA
GIORDANO
ZAMMUTO
DELUCIA
BALISTRIERI
ZERELLI
GIANCANO
MAGADDINO

SCALISH
GENOVESE
LAROCCA
CANTENA

PATRIARCA
ROA
CORALLO
TRAMUNTI
GAMBINO
COLOMBO
SCIACCA
DECAVALCANTE
REILA
BRUNO

LANSKY
TRAFFICANTE
MARCELLO

Information gathering at the local level secures information from these basic sources:

Published facts and information about the involvement of persons in illegal activities. This information is from newspapers, magazines, and correspondence between police agencies.

Information between an officer and informant. In actual practice, the use of this information is too selective and should be expanded to include *all* field officers. An informer who is to be used more than once should be identified and his name (or code name) kept in the file of the vice commander.

The initiation of investigations to gain information and to gather evidence for criminal prosecution. This may encourage the use of the "paid informer" and other techniques.

The paid informer, if properly supervised, can contribute to the solution of many cases. The officer using a paid informer should:

Be sure the crime is of sufficient magnitude to warrant the expenditure.

See that all information received is channeled to appropriate units for further investigation.

Screen informers carefully; make sure motives for informing are legal.

Make the informer aware of the laws governing "entrapment."

Be aware that the informer may also be wanting information. An informer will frequently have divided loyalties.

Attempt to validate the authenticity of the information. If this is not possible, a notation should show other investigators that the information has not been validated.

Exercise caution in entering into a permanent file information that has not been validated or is questionable as to its reliability.

The use of a "police operator" or "undercover officer" is an effective method for securing certain types of informa-

Organization and Internal Communications for Enforcement

tion. The police officer, posing as an informer, may be used effectively in the following ways:

To observe and report on activities that he may see on the street.

To solicit information from contacts on the street who do not know that he is a police officer.

To follow up and verify leads that are fed to him by field officers.

To seek out persons who actively engage in the planning of criminal activity so that information from and about them may be reported back to the regular enforcement officers.

To report situations of importance that reflect upon the enforcement effort of the department.

How a Records System
Should Function

An illustration as to how such a system might work is shown in the following examples. Information in an automated records system will be entered from the following sources:

Information from an event or an occurrence will enter the system from a simplified form called the Event Report Cue Sheet (see Appendix I).

Information on suspects and subject under investigation will be taken from a simplified complaint form called the People Cue Sheet (see Appendix I).

Information on an arrestee, location, and type of crime will come from booking records on the Booking Report Cue Sheet (see Appendix I).

License and permit information will automatically be entered from agencies concerned with a license. (For example, the City Clerk's Office issues all business licenses. Information on ownership, type of business, etc., would automatically be entered into the computer system.)

For an automated vice-reporting and records system, the following minimum requirements should be designed into the system to be utilized by the field officer:

An on-line system should be implemented so that immediate retrieval is possible.

The flexibility for expanding into state and federal systems should be in the basic planning. A fairly sophisticated records systems can be maintained with unit record equipment only.

Historical events and unsolved crimes attributed to organized and vice-related criminals should be programmed and entered into the system.

Methods of operations currently being utilized by the organized criminal should become a part of the system.

Location files, such as suspected gambling locations, should become a part of the system. Inquiry on a given location will automatically print out a complete background file. This will be good information to establish probable cause.

Current photographs and known associates taken from interview cards (much like the field interrogation card) will project each department officer into the intelligence-gathering process.

Vice complaints coming to the investigator will be automatically checked against past complaints at the location and suspects named will have a national check made against their past activities. In addition, utility hook-ups, business licenses, permits, and vehicles registered to any involved suspect will be automatically checked prior to an investigation.

Vice records will no longer be separate files but will be a part of an integrated criminal justice system. Records of a confidential nature, in the data processing system, will be more secure than is now possible in a manual records system. Remote inquiry stations can be programmed to receive only specific information; thus, the central storage unit can be protected against indiscriminate inquiry and will even note the source of an unauthorized inquiry.[3]

The building of speed and flexibilty into vice intelligence records systems will be one of the significant advancements in vice control in the next decade. Direct access to past police history, methods of operation, and current illegal activities

[3]Statement in a training session by Mr. Richard E. McDonnell, Manager, Law Enforcement and Criminal Justice Activities, I.B.M., Homestead, Poughkeepsie, New York, April 23, 1968.

Organization and Internal Communications for Enforcement

Table 2–1
The Intelligence System

Information (Varied Sources)		Evaluation (Conversion)		Intelligence (Conclusion)		Dissemination (Action)		Feedback
The gathering of the raw information should come from all sources and segments of the community. The nature of the information should be recorded and compared with other data.	=	In the comparison and the comprehension, at least these five criteria should be applied: 1. Reliability of the source; 2. Validity of the information; 3. Extent to which the information can be supported through other methods; 4. Usefulness; 5. Timeliness.	=	The information having been evaluated, it must now be considered intelligence and must be stated in the form of conclusive expressions with supported predictions that lend themselves to preventive or prosecutive action.	=	The intelligence must be transmitted accurately and swiftly to the unit responsible for enforcement.	=	The source of the information ultimately must be advised of the outcome of the information. Frequently the officer who provides information never hears of any results and may develop a reluctance to actively seek out and report information.

15

for use in vice investigations will support better prosecutions and improve the information system. The ability to secure immediate information on transient vice violators will bring together pertinent data from many areas.

The Intelligence Gathering Process as a Part of the Vice Records System. The intelligence process, as it relates to record keeping functions, is identified by Lieutenant Robert Earhart, Michigan State Police, in this manner:

> The scope of the information must cover past, present and proposed criminal and disruptive activities, to provide two basic types of positive action. The first is preventive and the second is prosecutive.[4]

Our examination of the intelligence function makes it evident that criminal intelligence is a process rather than an entity in itself, as can be readily seen in Table 2–1.

The officer is only as good as his information sources and he is frequently reluctant to seek information through official channels. In addition to his precinct or division files, the officer should freely utilize intelligence files from the field patrol and from related agencies of the city, county, and state.

The vice division is one of the key sub-units of the department that both generates and utilizes intelligence information; thus, it is imperative that an officer be willing to contribute to the system and utilize the information feedback in his enforcement work.

In Chapter III some problems in dealing with the legal system are shown.

[4]Robert Earhart, "Intelligence Gathering, Evaluation, Dissemination and Surveillance," A Monograph (Lansing, Michigan: Department of State Police, 1969).

Through administrative proceedings and judicial decisions, the legal system offers a great deal of assistance for a successful vice law enforcement program. Activities that will assist the field officer are: (1) decisions and policies made by city administrative commissions; (2) selected case decisions of the trial and appellate courts; and (3) the maintaining of good judicial relations.

Decisions and Policies Made by Administrative Commissions

There are basically two types of commissions that will have an impact upon the vice conditions of a community: state or regional commissions and police commissions (see Fig. 3–1).

State or Regional Crime Commissions

The crime commission composed of lay citizens can be of service to a field officer in the following ways. It can:

Reveal any lack of enforcement and prosecution of vice conditions.

Furnish information to law enforcement agencies. (Frequently citizens will come to a crime commission with information they would not give to the police.)

Do research on the structure of criminal groups and their activities.

Serve as an educational medium in meeting with and trans-

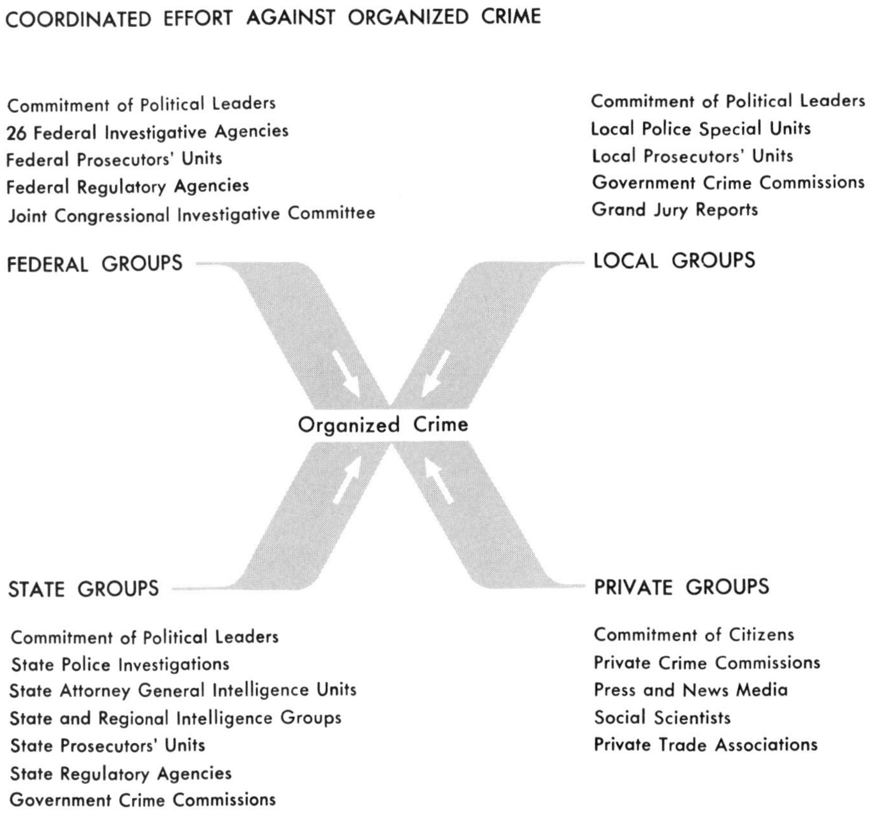

Commitment of Political Leaders
26 Federal Investigative Agencies
Federal Prosecutors' Units
Federal Regulatory Agencies
Joint Congressional Investigative Committee

Commitment of Political Leaders
Local Police Special Units
Local Prosecutors' Units
Government Crime Commissions
Grand Jury Reports

FEDERAL GROUPS ————————————— LOCAL GROUPS

Organized Crime

STATE GROUPS ————————————— PRIVATE GROUPS

Commitment of Political Leaders
State Police Investigations
State Attorney General Intelligence Units
State and Regional Intelligence Groups
State Prosecutors' Units
State Regulatory Agencies
Government Crime Commissions

Commitment of Citizens
Private Crime Commissions
Press and News Media
Social Scientists
Private Trade Associations

Fig. 3–1. Group effort in the fight against organized crime. From the President's Task Force report on organized crime.

mitting information concerning organized crime to the community.

The basis for crime commission operations is fairly obscure and their relationships to other elements of the legal structure have not been resolved.

In general, crime commissions serve as a check upon all governmental operations including the grand jury. The commission is not usually a governmental agency and its financial position is always in question. The 1968 Omnibus Crime Bill which provides for a government-sponsored agency may make

The Legal System and Vice Control

the crime commission concept a reality in many areas of the country.

Police Commissions

A police commission is a lay group that is usually appointed by the political party in power for the purpose of making broad policy decisions for the operation of a police department. In some instances the police commission is the administrative subunit that has the responsibility for issuing licenses and permits to businesses that are susceptible to control by organized criminal groups. The commission frequently sits as an administrative tribunal in exercising licensing control over such potential vice related activities as live entertainment in public establishments, the regulation of taxi drivers, photography studios, bath houses, and other places.

The importance of the police commission as a licensing agency in controlling potential vice locations, activities, and suspects should not be overlooked by the police investigator. If properly used, the commission is of substantial assistance to a law enforcement unit.

Commissions of either type operate primarily by making conditions regarding organized crime known. Publicity of this type can be a valuable community resource.

Case Decisions of the Trial and Appellate Courts Influencing Vice Operations

By familiarizing himself with a few select court cases pertaining to legal procedures used in vice enforcement, the officer can establish a framework within which to operate. Cases that pertain to issues that arise in vice enforcement are cited in these cases.

The Exclusionary Rule. Evidence must be legally seized to be admissible in court. *Mapp v. Ohio*, 367 U.S. 643 (1961).

Evidence Obtained with Listening Devices. Electronic eavesdropping (e.g., wiretapping), where a trespass takes place, is subject to a search warrant. *Katz v. U.S.,* 389 U.S. 347 (1967).

Where a person carries a recording instrument on his person and there is no trespass, a warrant is not required. *Topez v. U.S.,* 373 U.S. 427 (1963).

Evidence obtained in violation of Section 605, Federal Communications Act, is inadmissible in state cases. *Lee v. Florida,* 389 U.S. 347 (1967).

In this highly critical area and where laws vary from state to state, a general rule would be to obtain a search warrant in every case possible.

Use of Informer Information.[5] Information given by a confidential, reliable informant may be sufficient without revealing name of informant. *McCray v. Illinois,* 386 U.S. 306 (1967). Officers made arrest on the basis of information given them by a confidential informer. Officers declined to identify informant. They had known and used informant for approximately one year. During that period he had *given accurate information at least fifteen or sixteen times and it had led to numerous convictions.* Conviction affirmed.

An officer should provide an independent investigation, when possible, to substantiate the information received from an informant.

Pre- and Post-Arrest Procedures. If statements are to be used as evidence (and they frequently are in vice cases), procedures should be based upon the following cases.

When the process becomes accusatory rather than investigatory, the officer must inform the accused of: (1) his right to remain silent; (2) his right to consultation with his attorney. *Escobedo v. Illinois,* 378 U.S. 478 (1964). The pre-interrogation warnings were carried over to both the *Dorado* 62 Cal. 2nd 338 (1965) and the *Miranda* 384 U.S. 436 (1966) decisions. The *Kent* 383 U.S. 541 (1965) and *Gault* 99 Ariz. 407 p 2d 760 (1965) cases reaffirm these and other rights for the juvenile.

[5]Liaison, Alameda County Sheriff's Department, Vol. XVI, No. 2 (January 22, 1969). Cases cited in this appendix were in part abstracted from this document. The cases were from the *Journal of California Law Enforcement,* Vol. 3, No. 3 (January, 1969).

The Legal System and Vice Control

Local Ordinances Not to Preempt State Law. Officers enforcing vice statutes are finding overlapping in state and local laws. In *Lane v. City of Los Angeles*, 58 Cal. 2nd 99 (1962), the court held that the state has adopted a general scheme for regulation of the criminal aspects of sexual activity. The court emphasized that local ordinances are invalid if they attempt to impose additional requirements in a field preempted by state law. (Refer to individual state statutes.)

Conduct of Entry with Warrant. Officers acting on both a regular warrant and a search warrant to secure lottery evidence and make arrest went to the defendant's house. They knocked on the door, waited twenty seconds, forced the door, and entered. No evidence was introduced to indicate that the defendant was attempting to flee or destroy evidence. The court in *Commonwealth (Penn.) v. Newman*, 240 A 2d 795 (1968), held that officers should make proper notification as to office and purpose of visit.

Maintaining Good Judicial Relations

An officer deals closely with the judiciary. There are often distinct conflicts that must be reconciled before an officer can be effective in vice prevention and enforcement. Some of the points of conflict to be reconciled are:

Many courts look upon vice type crimes as a nuisance. Some types of violations are harshly dealt with while others equally structured in law are ignored.

Because of individual philosophies or for the public good, prosecutions may be terminated.

The court-prosecutor-defense triangle makes many arbitrary decisions for dismissals, adjustments of penalty, etc., without consultation with arresting or investigating officers as to the background of the defendant.

In order to avoid conflicts, it is suggested that the officer:

Disassociate himself emotionally from the case being tried. The sentence imposed or the disposition in a case should be of limited concern to the officer. This does not imply that the officer, through the media available and as a private citizen, should not actively campaign for necessary change.

Prepare cases and reports in such a precise manner that there is no legal question concerning the case.

Review notes on each case prior to court testimony. It is easy for an officer handling many cases to become confused over similar incidents.

Become acquainted with the prosecutor and his techniques for presenting a case.

Not show concern regarding the court's philosophy about vice crimes.

Be neutral in his opinions and expressions about certain types of vice violators. The court or jury can detect antagonistic attitudes.

The relationship an officer establishes with the court is important. If there is an expression of a differing professional opinion, the officer should ask to confer with the prosecutor or the judge outside of the courtroom.

The Legal System and Vice Control

A basic ingredient of a good vice law enforcement program is a set of general policy statements detailing how personnel shall function. Because of the sensitive nature of vice law enforcement, all officers should be directed by the same policy. Department manuals should include: (1) general guidelines and (2) guidelines pertaining to expense accounting.

General Guidelines

All vice laws should be strictly enforced.

Vice violations, although different from other crimes, should be an enforcement function of *all* officers.

The techniques of enforcement should be within the rule of law. Sensational or emotional crimes do not justify deviation from the legal laws of arrest.

An officer in the field cannot moralize. The statutory laws are explicit and serve as his guide.

All violations reported to a department should be reduced to writing. All investigations made should be recorded in writing as the investigation progresses.

Records should be protected but should not be so secretive as to render the information useless.

The complexity of vice law enforcement creates special problems which should be brought to the attention of the officer. The following points tend to illustrate why vice control does not respond to normal enforcement practices.[1]

[1] Denny F. Pace and Jimmie C. Styles, *"The Dynamics of Vice Control"* (Unpublished Manuscript, Kent State University, Kent, Ohio, 1969).

chapter

4

The procedures for the investigation of vice crimes are unlike those for a regular crime. The use of an operator or of expensive surveillance is frequently the only way in which a crime can be solved. The investigations in vice activities are commonly conducted over longer periods of time than other investigations.

If the police or undercover operator must participate, this can be a slow, tedious procedure for gathering evidence.

Undercover operators need funds for extensive investigations. At the local level these funds are not usually adequate.

Leaders of the crime syndicates tend to split operations between cities and states; thus, a complete picture of the operation is unknown to the local officer.

Participating criminals will frequently transfer their activities, causing local officers to lose contact with the violators and informants.

There is great overlapping of crime syndicates into legitimate businesses; laws are not adequate to cover borderline cases.

Local police agencies lack wide jurisdiction. The authority to investigate certain types of crimes should be statewide.

There is a failure to impose available sanctions through licensing and permits. Background investigations on many types of businesses prove to be helpful in keeping the criminal element to a minimum.

The legislature fails to make and update laws to meet the changing needs of society. State procedural law tends to lag years behind Supreme Court decisions.

The courts often fail to rigidly enforce existing laws and the use of probation and parole procedures is often lax.

There is a dismal lack of public concern toward such crimes.

Local departments neglect to acknowledge the existence of organized crime and to educate the public regarding its presence.

Guidelines Pertaining to Expenses

Any officer is responsible for the expenditure of money supplied to him from official sources to conduct investigations. The expenditure of and accounting for this money require that, for every dollar spent, there must be:

A signed receipt from the expending officer;

A designation of the amount spent;

The reason for the expenditure;

Any complaints, arrests, or other case dispositions made as a result of the expenditure.[2]

Contrary to popular belief, most money expended for information at the local level is spent in small amounts for cigarettes, sandwiches, and candy bars for hungry informants. Consequently, if good information is going to come from the informant over long periods of time, it is important that the officer keep the expenditure in proportion to the information received.

Unit commanders usually have some latitude in determining how the money is spent; however, the field officer is responsible for the expenditure of "secret service money" and for providing the records for audit. A favorite target of political office-seekers is auditing the expenditure of these funds.

In Chapter 5 an overview of organized crime is presented. Before an officer can understand the vested interests of small-time violators, he must see their relationships to the organized criminal groups. Through an understanding of vice intelligence processes, this relationship may be shown.

[2]International City Managers' Association, *Municipal Police Administration*, 6th ed. (Chicago: I.C.M.A., 1969).

Organized Crime

There is substantial evidence that criminal syndicates are involved in vice crimes. While many vice violations are the result of individual weaknesses, findings from various congressional subcommittees indicate rather clearly that organization among vice criminals is common.

Police contact with organized crime historically has been reserved for specialized units. Because of this procedure the field officer is unaware of what is happening around him. Information that should be known to *all* police officers has not been properly analyzed and communicated to the field officer. Conversely, information that may be valuable to the control of organized crime, and specifically vice, is lost because the field officer has not become a part of the intelligence-gathering process.

The question of police control of organized vice has long ago given way to a policy of coexistence. Departments have found that specialized units to control organized elements are largely ineffective because of the vast scope of the criminal operations. Specialized units, while important for documenting movements of individuals in the organized confederations, cannot control them. The best that can be expected from the specialized units is to make *all* officers of the department aware that such organizations exist. In order to create this awareness, an understanding of the following is essential: (1) the symptoms of organized crime; (2) the role of the federal government; and (3) the structure of organized confederations and how to recognize them.

Symptoms of Organized Crime

The direct link between vice activity and organized criminal groups is frequently difficult to show and almost impossible to prove. Activities of vice confederations are so covert that it is impossible to detect them through normal investigative methods.[1]

Frequently, the results and implications of a crime involving suspects belonging to organized groups will not be clearly established until years later. Because of the fluidity and the secretiveness of these crimes, an immediate evaluation by the police investigator may be based upon no more than conjecture. This is not to fault the police agency because individual guarantees under law may make a complete investigation impossible. Immediate and admissible facts involving elements of an organized vice group are rare.[2]

The Task Force Report on organized crime identifies some problems for the field investigator. To summarize these, one may conclude that:

> The core of organized crime is the supplying of illegal goods and services, but it is also deeply involved in legitimate business.

> Organized crime wants power and money and the procedures used to obtain them will be those which it devises to administer summarily and invisibly.

> Much of the money organized crime accumulates comes from innumerable petty transactions.

> Sometimes the activities of organized crime do not directly affect individuals.

> The purpose of organized crime is not competition with visible, legal government, but nullification of it.

> Organization, by centralizing power, systematizes a method of corrupting the law enforcement processes.

> Business ownership is easily concealed and businesses frequently do not take care in identifying the persons with whom they deal.

> Methods for enforcing organization edicts are moving from outright personal violence to coercion and blackmail which, in most instances, are just as effective.

> Today's corruption is less visible, more subtle, and, therefore, more difficult to detect and assess than in past times.

> A city need not be controlled by organized crime for its

[1] Denny F. Pace and Jimmie C. Styles, "The Dynamics of Vice Control" (Unpublished Manuscript, Kent State University, Kent, Ohio, 1969).
[2] Ibid.

Symptoms of Organized Crime

enforcement agencies to be ineffective. A few key positions in mid-management can render a department ineffective.

In-depth knowledge of local organizations should be obtained so that legal action may be initiated.[3]

Federal Participation in Vice Control and Its Stated Objectives

The participation of the federal government in the attack upon organized crime is necessary because of the scope and power of the national confederations of organized criminals. The use of federal resources is the only way in which the community can hope to limit the influences of the criminal confederations. The actual participation of the federal agencies need to be not only of a coordinating nature but of active participation with local and regional police agencies.

Past efforts of the federal agencies have been limited. The Nixon administration, in expanding upon the recommendations of the 1967 President's Crime Commission, has begun to implement many of the recommendations for the control of organized crime. These recommendations are cited in Appendix II.

Structure of the Organized Confederations and How to Recognize Them

Organized criminal activities involve many areas of the business community; however, the emphasis in this handbook is on vice activities.

A *confederation* implies an organization conducting activities under a coordinated plan of action. The Oyster Bay

---

[3]The President's Commission on Law Enforcement and Administration of Justice, *Task Force Report: Organized Crime* (Washington, D.C.: U.S. Government Printing Office, 1967).

Organized Crime

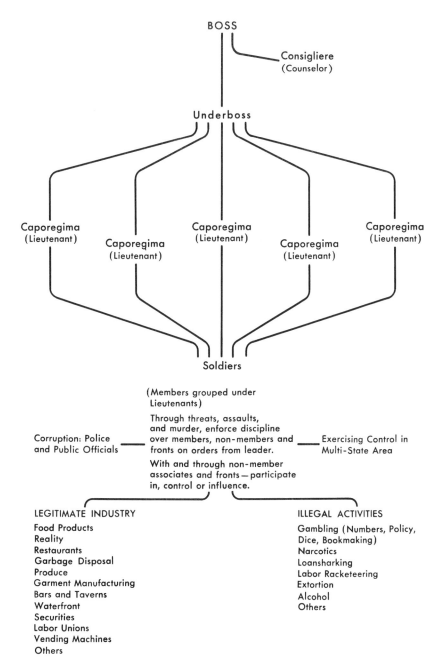

BOSS

Consigliere
(Counselor)

Underboss

Caporegima
(Lieutenant)

Caporegima
(Lieutenant)

Caporegima
(Lieutenant)

Caporegima
(Lieutenant)

Caporegima
(Lieutenant)

Soldiers

(Members grouped under
Lieutenants)

Corruption: Police
and Public Officials

Through threats, assaults,
and murder, enforce discipline
over members, non-members and
fronts on orders from leader.

Exercising Control in
Multi-State Area

With and through non-member
associates and fronts — participate
in, control or influence.

LEGITIMATE INDUSTRY

Food Products
Reality
Restaurants
Garbage Disposal
Produce
Garment Manufacturing
Bars and Taverns
Waterfront
Securities
Labor Unions
Vending Machines
Others

ILLEGAL ACTIVITIES

Gambling (Numbers, Policy,
Dice, Bookmaking)
Narcotics
Loansharking
Labor Racketeering
Extortion
Alcohol
Others

Fig. 5–1. An organized crime family. From the President's Crime Commission
report on organized crime, p. 9.

Report identifies some of the common elements of the so-called syndicate groups.[4]

> There is an unlawful conspiracy between two or more persons.
>
> The agreement may be actual or implied.
>
> There is a semi-permanency in its form, much like the modern corporation.
>
> The organizational structures are in a continuous "fluid transition" to compensate for political and criminal misfortunes of its members.
>
> The regional organizations are heteronomous; thus, the fear, corruption, totalitarian influences, and the insulation of leadership have a common pattern throughout the United States and even in many other areas of the world.
>
> The type of organizational control varies with the charismatic personalities of individual leaders. Control can be authoritarian or a loose knit laissez-faire structure. Either may be equally effective.

Activities frequently may be contrary to good public policy, yet they may not constitute a crime (see Fig. 5–1).

A weakness of many American police systems, with reference to vice activities, is the failure of police administrators to make *all* of their officers aware of the impact of the corner bookie, the small gambling games of an organized nature, and other minor violations that fit into schemes of the confederations. The police administrator, perhaps because of lack of information, has not stressed the deleterious effect that small local organized activities can have upon the entire operation of a law enforcement system.

The following chapter identifies some specific local gambling problems and indicates how the laws against these violations may be enforced by local police officers.

[4]*Combating Organized Crime,* A Report of the 1965 Oyster Bay, New York, Conferences (Albany, N.Y.: Office of the Counsel to the Governor, 1965), pp. 18–24.

Organized Crime

Gambling

Gambling in its many forms is one of the most frequent vice violations requiring police attention. Because of its widespread popularity and frequency, gambling is one of the mainstays of organized crime; thus, a major effort of any department is directed toward the suppression of gaming activities. The major problems of illegal gambling are: (1) bookmaking; (2) lotteries; and (3) cards and dice.

Bookmaking

"Bookmaking," "pool-selling," and "wagering" are all terms that describe the transaction of making a bet. Because of the relationship of gambling to organized crime syndicates, federal gambling laws are being used with increased frequency.

Federal Gambling Laws

Title 18 of the U.S. Code, Section 1084 specifies that it is a federal felony for anyone:

To engage in the business of betting or wagering.

To knowingly use a wire communication facility for the transmission of gambling information in interstate or foreign commerce, including bets or wagers, information assisting in the placing of bets on any sporting event or contest which entitles the recipient to receive money or credit as a result of bets or wagers, or any information assisting in any of the above.

Section 7302 Internal Revenue Code specifies that:

chapter

6

A vehicle may be seized if a gambler carries paraphernalia or conducts gambling operations in the vehicle. Obtain statements connecting vehicle to gambling during arrest and impound. Notify Intelligence Division, I.R.S.

An officer may use Section 1084 U.S. Code or an applicable state law to have phones removed from gambling locations. A law enforcement agency may notify the communications company whose facilities are being used to facilitate gambling, and service to the violator will be discontinued. *Notification must be made in writing.*

Communications using special carriers are also prohibited. Title 18 U.S. Code, Section 1953, states:

> It is a federal felony for anyone except a common carrier in the normal course of business to knowingly carry or send in interstate or foreign commerce any record, paraphernalia, ticket, certificate, bill, slip, token [involved in gambling activities].

Bookmaking is usually regulated under state law. Chapter 2915 of the Ohio Revised Code includes these subsections:

> 2915.06—No person shall play a game for money or other thing of value.
>
> 2915.09—No person shall keep a room or building, or portion thereof, or occupy public or private grounds with apparatus, books, or other devices for recording wagers or selling pools.

These crimes are misdemeanors.

In 1970 New York state legalized off-track betting. Las Vegas has long had parimutuel parlors where off-track betting could be conducted. These states assess a tax on the wagers being made. State operated betting is not subject to federal taxation. In most states bookmaking is a felony. Insert the law pertaining to bookmaking in your state.

State Statutes on Bookmaking

_____

_____

Gambling

Bookmaking is the most highly organized of all vice crimes; the extent of the organization is shown in Figure 6–1.[1] Without peripheral services such as wire services, the ability to lay off bets, and the protection that comes from the organization, the nationwide system could not exist.

[1] Denny F. Pace and Jimmie C. Styles, "The Dynamics of Vice Control" (Unpublished Manuscript, Kent State University, Kent, Ohio, 1969).

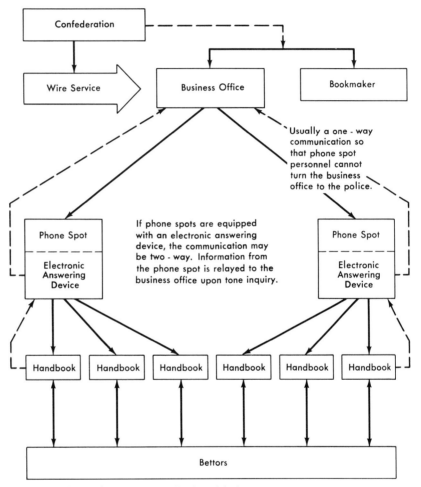

Contact between the handbook and the bettor may or may not be a two - way operation. This is usually the weakest link in the bookmaking operation and the confederations have handbooks that are expendable.

Fig. 6–1.   The bookmaking empire.

Federal laws have forced the wire services to operate behind legitimate business fronts. Bookmaking information still comes to the local bookmakers through subscribed wire services and sports information networks.

In order to protect legitimate information from being intercepted and diverted to illegal uses, Title 47 U.S. Code 605 prohibits intercepting, divulging, publishing, or using any part of a communication. This statute may be used if legal communication lines are tapped by bookmakers for the purpose of securing gaming or racing information. This section does not apply when evidence is gained by legal monitoring under state law.

As illustrated in Figure 6–1, the use of electronic answering devices has put many bookmakers beyond the reach of local law enforcement.

An officer is in frequent contact with the "street corner bookie." The bookmaker at the street level will usually handle either horse action or action on football, baseball, and other events.

"Horse" and other bookies may be specialized according to the following patterns of operation. The type of investigation to be conducted for their apprehension will depend upon the operating pattern of the individual bookie.

The Handbook. (See Fig. 6–2.) His method of operation will depend upon the established, successful techniques he has carefully perfected. In order to legally arrest the handbook, the investigator must do one of the following:

Use an operator to make a bet with the handbook.
Receive reliable information to establish probable cause for arrest.
Observe the bookie until a pattern of operation has been established and the investigator has reasonable cause to believe a crime is being committed.

The most difficult handbook to apprehend under present police operating methods is the one who commits all bets to memory. After several bets are taken, he then calls his "office" (see Fig. 6–3). The office in turn reduces the bets from memory to writing. These handbooks do not specialize in any particular pattern of operation but may be found in any of the following categories:

Gambling

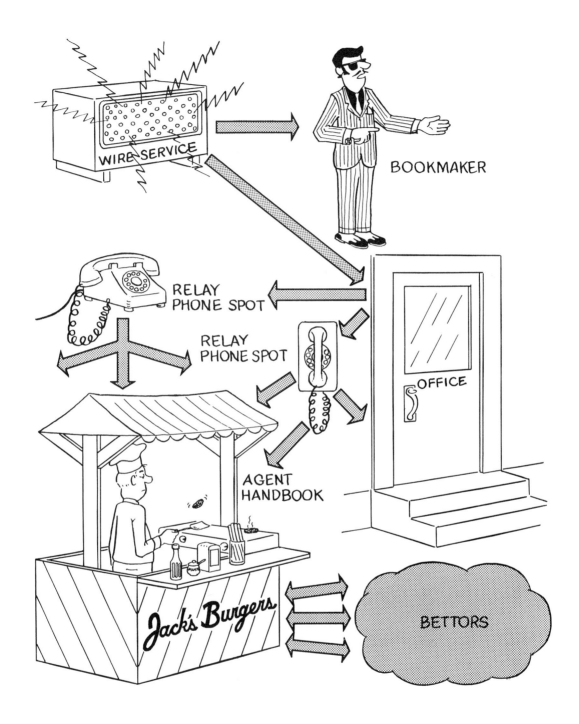

Fig. 6–2. A typical bookmaking operation.

Fig. 6–3. A handbook utilizing a public phone to contact his "office."

THE EMPLOYEE. The bookie who is an employee of a firm where his regular duties put him in contact with other employees—e.g., a toolman, union representative, etc.

THE FIXED SPOT. He usually operates from a newsstand, cigar or candy store where it is normal for a number of persons to gather without being conspicuous.

THE TRAVELER. This bookie runs routes from bar to bar, accepts bets from patrons of cafes on his route and will be found where people regularly gather.

Whatever the handbook's technique, he is usually smart and well-disciplined in not having materials in his possession that may serve as evidence. The handbook is clever and difficult to apprehend. How the handbook working phones avoids apprehension may be shown in Figure 6–4. When officers enter to search the room where the telephone is registered the bookie has sufficient time to destroy the evidence and abandon the wired-out telephone.

Evidence Necessary for Prosecution. Betting markers or slips usually furnish the most obvious evidence of bookmaking activity. These may be simple scrawled notations or highly sophisticated codes. The officer should be able to

Gambling

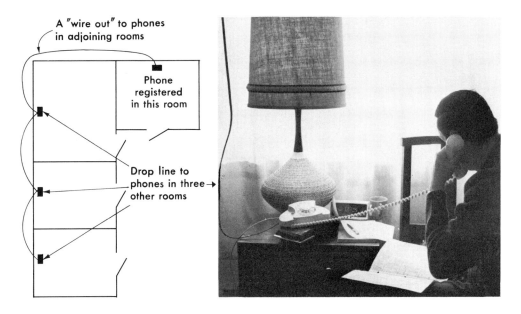

A "wire out" to phones in adjoining rooms

Phone registered in this room

Drop line to phones in three → other rooms

Fig. 6-4. A phone spot with a "wire out" to phones installed in adjoining rooms.

rial or object is called a *betting marker* and may range from a small slip of paper to a ceramic tile. It will usually be an object that can be quickly destroyed or from which notations can be easily erased. The production of this object in court with appropriate notations, deciphered as betting notations, is required for most convictions. The *National Daily Reporter* is frequently found on bookies and bettors. It may be interpreted as a betting marker if notations are made on the publication.

The following are usually required for the arrest of the bookmaker:

> Probable cause for arrest based upon reliable information plus an independent investigation which supports the information that a crime is being committed.
>
> If the reliable informant is produced in court, the inde-

Bookmaking

Interpretation

The bettor
6th race
Santa Anita Race Track
The horse
$2 to show

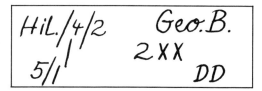

The bettor
4th race
Hialeah Race Track
2nd post position
If horse wins bet
Parlays to horse in
5th race 1st pole
Position
$2 to win

Hap				Schizo	
SA 6 JK			2	2	
Hil 4/2	2			2	
HP 2/4	2	2	②	6	6.80
GG. 1/7	10			10	
				20	6.80
				+13.20	

Hap is the agent
Schizo is the bettor

Information from
above markers to
indicate the track,
the race, the horse
and the amount wagered

This record shows a
total of $20 bet and
a payoff of $6.80 or
a profit of $13.20

This may be a daily
or weekly record

Fig. 6–5. Typical betting markers with interpretation and the professional betting marker found at phone spots and offices to record action.

pendent investigation may be minimized or, in some instances, eliminated.

Evidence such as a betting marker to substantiate and confirm what the investigator may see and hear (see **Fig. 6–6**).

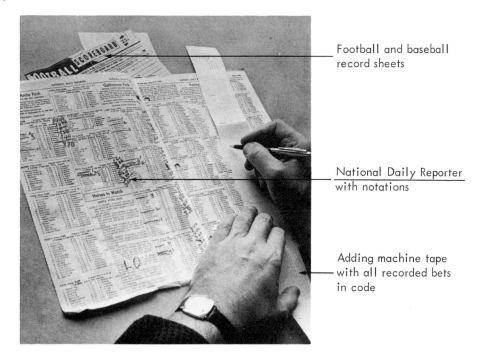

Football and baseball record sheets

National Daily Reporter with notations

Adding machine tape with all recorded bets in code

Fig. 6–6. Typical paraphernalia with notations to indicate that wagering is taking place.

Testimony of overt actions which indicates that the bookie is actually taking bets—e.g., he is approached by known bettors, he consults with a racing form, and there is a transaction of money (see Fig. 6–7).

In some states venue for the crime must be shown.

In addition to the wire services, an important ingredient to the bookmaking enterprise is the odds maker. The odds maker utilizing the Totalizor Board, found at all major tracks, establishes the payoff rates for the street bookie.

Parimutuel Machines and Betting Odds. The tracks throughout the country all have "tote boards" that give odds

Bookmaking

NATIONAL DAILY REPORTER

Pimlico

— OFFICIAL JOCKEYS AND POST POSITIONS —
Percentage of winning favorites corresponding meeting 1965, .36; current meeting, .30. Percentage of favorites in the money, .59. Daily double on first and second races. United starting gate. Confirmation camera.

★ Indicates beaten favorite last time out.
Horses listed in order as handicapped by **EL RIO REY**

WEATHER CLEAR—TRACK FAST

FIRST—Purse, $3,300   Probable POST 10:00 A. M.
1 1-8 Miles. 4-Year-Olds and Up. Claiming
Colts and Geldings

Hcp.		Last Finish	Wt.	P.P.	Prob. Odds	Jockey
1	§Red Erik	6 113	11		3-1	R.Adams
2	Beech Time	3 116	14		7-2	G.Patterson
3	News Wire	4 116*18			4-1	C.Baltazar
6	Keb	5 122	6		5-1	J.Brocklebank
8	Friendly Cat	9 116	1		8-1	W.J.Passmore
9	Milrutho	3 116	7		8-1	J.Block
10	Even Swap	7 116	10		12-1	C.F.Riston
11	Sterling Prince	116	12		15-1	R.J.Bright
12	*Mr. Songster	9 107	15		20-1	E.Belville
13	‡Jambar	9 109*	8		30-1	N.Reagan
16	‡Spider Spread	5 109	9		30-1	A.Garcia
17	Billy Giampa	12 116	4		30-1	R.McCurdy
4	Congratulations	1 122	17		——	SCRATCHED
5	Dumelle ★	5 119	16		——	SCRATCHED
7	Fast Answer	3 116	5		——	SCRATCHED
14	Regal Lover	6 116	3		——	SCRATCHED
15	Little Rib	10 116	13		——	SCRATCHED
18	Graf Smil	11 116×	2		——	SCRATCHED

SECOND—Purse, $3,300   Probable POST 10:26 A. M.
6 Furlongs. 3-Year-Olds. Claiming

1	Broken Needle	2 111×	1		2-1	G.Patterson
2	Woodlake Witch	111	5		4-1	P.Kallai
3	Lady Macbeth	11 117	7		5-1	F.Lovato
4	‡Mink Boy	6 109	8		6-1	R.Nolan
5	Craig's Fault	8 116	9		8-1	B.Phelps
6	Fast Lass	3 111 10			8-1	C.Baltazar
7	Tora Tora	10 116	11		8-1	P.I.Grimm
8	Hawkins	7 116*	3		10-1	T.Lee
13	*Carole A.	6			12-1	N.Reagan
14	Its a Star	9 116	4		15-1	T.Guyton
16	Mr. Cricket	11 116	12		30-1	R.Kimball
17	*Marv's Joy	10 111	2		30-1	J.Taylor
9	‡Blocker	— 109	14		——	SCRATCHED
10	Yokel	— 116	15		——	SCRATCHED
11	Drag Pit	— 116	16		——	SCRATCHED
12	Little Nancy	— 111	18		——	SCRATCHED
15	Ginnygem	8 111	13		——	SCRATCHED
18	Jovial Lady	12 111	17		——	SCRATCHED

THIRD—Purse, $3,300   Probable POST 10:52 A. M.
6 Furlongs. 3-Year-Olds. Claiming

Used for racing information by legitimate racetrack bettors. If notations are made, the reporter becomes a betting marker.

Fig. 6—7. The *National Daily Reporter*, a publication.

on the horse prior to the race based upon such factors as past racing records, work-out times, jockey, and the amount of money wagered by the bettors. The odds, as established by the tote boards, are recognized by the illegal off-track bookie up to 15 to 1 odds.

The bookie, in order to avoid fixes on "long shots" and "past postings,"[2] has generally settled on a maximum of 15 to 1 odds. Frequently, if the bookie likes a horse and the track odds are greater than 15 to 1, he will lay off his bets at the race track; in similar circumstances, the street bookie, for a 10 to 15 percent commission, will lay off to the big bookmaker, who in turn may use track wagering facilities.

Small bookies will generally lay off their bets to syndicate sponsored bookmakers. If the action gets too heavy, the syndicate man will, in turn, dump his bets at the track, which will in turn bring down those odds; thus, the track in fact serves as a hedge against big losses.

Bets enter the race track in many ways. For example, a syndicate bookmaker may hold bets until twenty to thirty minutes before race time, then send a runner into the track with money for the parimutuel windows. If the selected horse wins, the runner will contact a *stand-in* (a race track patron who is equipped with phony identification) who claims his winnings, settles his commitment to Internal Revenue, and returns the winnings to the syndicate runner for a fee.

Sports Betting. Betting on sports has surpassed the dollar amounts bet on horse races. Along with national television, the sports bookie has firmly established himself as a necessary commodity for the betting sports fan. Sports betting is lucrative for the syndicate because the syndicate can control the odds set on a game. The service is sold from regional locations—e.g., Houston, Las Vegas, Chicago and Seattle—and guides the odds set in the *opening sports line*. The purpose of handicapping is to make the weak team look strong or to temper the strength of the strong team.

The sports bookmaker does no gambling. In reality, he is a middleman working on a commission. He arranges to let the bettors bet against themselves. By adjusting the price line

---

[2]Past posting is the placing of bets after a race has been run and the winner decided. By delaying the transmission of the official results of a race to the "old-time" bookie, it was possible to place bets in this way on a horse that had already won. It is rarely done now.

Bookmaking

he quotes to bettors, he is able to deal himself in for from 5 to 10 percent. The bookmaker obtains information from the *initial line* which is established upon the relative merits of the team. The *final line* is then adjusted to the betting trends. The final line is adjusted to protect the "commission" for the bookmaker.

An example of the many devices to assist the sports bookmaker is shown in Figure 6–8.

Lotteries

The term *lottery* covers a large and varied number of schemes. Many will consist of innocent pastime gimmicks for entertainment and for raising money for worthy causes. Most, however, emanate from organizational schemes indicated in Figure 6–9.[3]

State laws are in fair agreement that a lottery involves three elements:

A scheme for the *disposal or distribution of property or prize*.

Participation by persons who have paid or promised to pay a valuable consideration.

Distribution determined by *lot or chance*.

Lottery laws are difficult to enforce because of the volume of lotteries and because of the variations in local statutes.

Federal laws covering lotteries are cited in Title 18 U.S. Code, Section 1301; these laws make it illegal to:

Bring into the United States, for the purpose of disposing of the same, or

Knowingly deposit with any express company or

Carry in interstate or foreign commerce, or

Knowingly take or receive (when so carried) any paper, certificate or instrument purporting to be or to represent a ticket, chance, share, or interest in or dependent upon the event of, a lottery, gift enterprise, or similar scheme, offering prizes dependent in whole or in part upon lot or chance or

[3]Pace and Styles, *op. cit.*

Gambling

Football Handicap

— NOT TO BE SOLD —

All Teams Must Win

TIES LOSE

You May Give or Take the Points

This card used as a business stimulant only. Not to be used as an inducement to wager.

3 Teams	5 Points
4 Teams	10 Points
5 Teams	15 Points
6 Teams	25 Points
7 Teams	40 Points
8 Teams	65 Points
10 Teams	100 Points
9 out of 10	20 Points Bonus

N⁰ 42902

- - - - - - - - - - - - - - - - - - -

N⁰ 42902

Name ....

....

Teams Picked.......................No.....................

CIRCLE TEAMS PLAINLY
GAMES FOR WEEK ENDING NOVEMBER

1. Rice	2. Texas A&M	+ 1
3. Florida State	4. No. Carolina St.	+ 3
5. Penn. State	6. Navy	+ 3
7. Georgia	8. Auburn	+ 3
9. Tennessee	10. Mississippi	+ 3
11. U.C.L.A.	12. Stanford	+ 6
13. Oregon	14. California	+ 6
15. Clemson	16. Maryland	+ 7
17. Texas Tech	18. Baylor	+ 7
19. Washington	20. Oregon St.	+ 7
21. L.S.U.	22. Mississippi State	+ 8
23. Purdue	24. Minnesota	+ 8
25. Michigan	26. Northwestern	+ 10
27. Ohio State	28. Iowa	+ 14
29. Missouri	30. Oklahoma	+ 14
31. Colorado	32. Kansas	+ 14
33. Arkansas	34. S.M.U.	+ 17
35. Texas	36. T.C.U.	+ 17
37. Georgia Tech	38. Virginia	+ 21
39. Alabama	40. So. Carolina	+ 21
41. Nebraska	42. Oklahoma St.	+ 24
43. U.S.C.	44. Pittsburgh	+ 24
45. Michigan St.	46. Indiana	+ 28
47. Notre Dame	48. No. Carolina	+ 30

PRO. GAMES

49. Washington	50. Philadelphia	+ 3
51. Baltimore	52. Minnesota	+ 3
53. Detroit	54. San Francisco	+ 7
55. Chicago	56. St. Louis	+ 7
57. Dallas	58. Pittsburgh	+ 7
59. Green Bay	60. Los Angeles	+ 13
61. Cleveland	62. New York Giants	+ 14

GAMES FOR WEEK ENDING NOVEMBER
CIRCLE TEAMS PLAINLY

1	2	3	4	5	6	7	8	9	10
11	12	13	14	15	16	17	18	19	20
21	22	23	24	25	26	27	28	29	30
31	32	33	34	35	36	37	38	39	40
41	42	43	44	45	46	47	48	49	50
51	52	53	54	55	56	57	58	59	60
61	62	63	64	65	66	67	68	69	70

Fig. 6–8. Example of sports gambling. Top half is retained by the bettor; the bottom half is removed and is forwarded to the confederation business office.

Any advertisement for or list of prizes drawn or awarded by means of such a lottery, etc.

Section 1302 prohibits as a misdemeanor the use of the mails to send any offer, ticket, money, money orders, etc., for

Lotteries

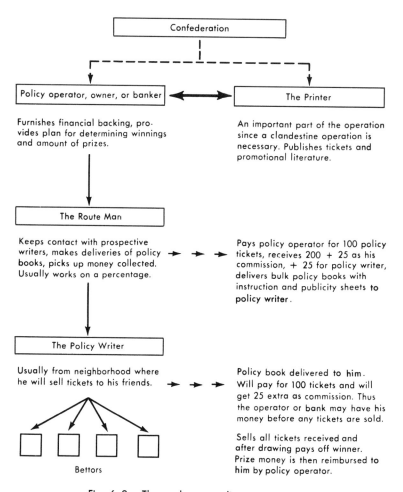

Fig. 6-9. The numbers or policy organization.

tickets or any newspaper or publication advertising lotteries or containing any list of any part or all of the prizes in a lottery.

Section 1304 prohibits as a misdemeanor the broadcasting of lottery information by radio stations.

Laws on numbers, policy, and lotteries are usually vested in state law. California Penal Code, Section 319 is broad in nature.[4] It says:

[4]Florida Statutes 849.09 prohibiting lottery, 849.01 prohibiting chain letters, pyramid clubs, etc., and 849.10 prohibiting the printing of lottery tickets agree in substance with this penal code section.

Gambling

A lottery is any scheme for the disposal or distribution of property by chance, among persons who have paid or promised to pay any valuable consideration for the chance of obtaining such property or a portion of it, for any share or any interest in such property, upon any agreement, understanding, or expectation that it is to be distributed or disposed of by lot or chance, or by whatever name the same may be known.

In Ohio the penalty for selling tickets for a lottery is given in the Revised Code 2915.10 (13063):

No person, for his own profit, shall vend, sell, barter, or dispose of a ticket, order or device for or representing a number of shares or an interest in a lottery or scheme of chance, by whatever name, style or title denominated or known, located in or to be drawn, paid or carried on within or without this state.

The possibility of dual interpretations of such a phrase as "for his own profit" creates many enforcement problems and establishes a double standard for the citizens of a community. In states where this provision is not made there are still ways to beat the lottery laws. "A lottery ticket is not sold," it is given in return for a donation; thus, the same subversion of the law is created. Cite the state or city law that applies to your department.

*State and Local
Lottery Laws*

Lotteries in Common Use.   Gas station gimmicks, bank night at the theater, and free door prizes are all examples of lotteries. *If a person is required to purchase anything in order to participate, the scheme qualifies as a lottery.* For example, if a person must buy gas to receive coupons for a drawing or must purchase a ticket to enter the movie house to participate in bank night or must purchase a ticket to be eligible for a door prize, then that person is participating in a lottery.

Baseball and Football Pools.   These pools are examples

Lotteries

Fig. 6–10.   The American Sweepstakes lottery scheme.

of the types of lotteries most commonly used by nonprofessional gamblers. Many that appear to be friendly, spontaneous pools are, however, professional pools that are sold and circulated by the syndicate.

Chain Letters, Pyramid Clubs, etc.   These schemes may be either professional or nonprofessional (Florida Statute 849.091).

Irish Sweepstakes.   This lottery is readily available in major metropolitan American cities. News media carry stories of big winners and so are instrumental in perpetuation of the lottery.

In recent years forgers have jumped in and produced counterfeit tickets. As a result, the chance of winning is further minimized because the buyer becomes the victim of a forgery scheme.

Gambling

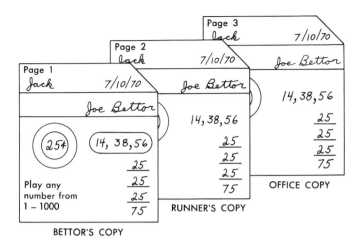

Fig. 6–11.   A typical lottery ticket sequence.

An example of a sweepstake-type lottery that was patterned after the Irish Sweepstakes was the one begun by the American Sweepstakes Corporation in Palmyra Island, American Polynesia, in 1965 (see Fig. 6–10). This lottery was short-lived, coming to an end when the promoters were prosecuted under federal lottery laws.

Numbers Game.   The numbers game is a pure lottery; only the methods of conducting the sale and pay-offs are different.

Sale of Professional Numbers Tickets.   The more exotic the scheme, the better the sale of tickets. Sale price of popular numbers games range from twenty-five cents to two dollars depending upon the neighborhood in which they are to be sold and the type of scheme involved. Basically a numbers ticket has three parts. The most common ticket type is three carbon copies in a booklet (see Fig. 6–11).

A professional organization will develop numbers, policy bolita, and dozens of other variations. The lotteries developed will arrange pay-offs that are based on ship docking time, time passed over the equator, stock exchange numbers, races, and the simplest of all—merely selecting a number and declaring a winner.

The winners in a numbers game will be assigned a given percentage of the sales. The promoters have a fixed share; thus, the only possible losers are the bettors.

Lotteries

a. Wood stacked against a newly constructed wall of a gambling location makes the building appear abandoned.

b. An unusual number of vehicles around this house indicates gambling may be in progress.

c. If the game is not familiar, have a player explain the details.

Photographs courtesy of Walnut Creek, California, Police Department.

Fig. 6–12. Common problems that arise in making gambling arrests.

Cards and Dice

Cards and dice are popular instruments for illicit gambling. Because they are mobile and simple to use, these instruments are well-known gaming devices.

Cards

Cards lend themselves well to house run games. House games may charge a fee to enter. Play at the table is free. In other games, the house collects periodically from individual tables or all players play against the house. Each state has its own laws prohibiting certain games. Florida Statute 849.08 prohibits cards, keno, roulette, faro, or other games of chance at any place, by any device. California Penal Code Section 330 prohibits card games except for draw poker, which is granted local option. New York Penal Code Section 970–4 a, b, c prohibits the "common gambler" from participation. Games for amusement and recreation only are not violations under the New York Law. Cite the laws that apply to your state.

State and Local Law Regarding Cards, etc. _____

_____

_____

Gambling

 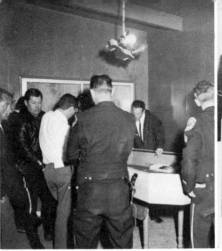 

d. Locate positions of players around the table and photograph the scene as it was observed.

e. There must be plenty of man-power to cover exits and secure all evidence.

f. A typical portable dice layout.

State and Local Law on "Visiting" where Gambling is Being Conducted. _____

_____

_____

The general rule is: Any card game based upon chance, not skill, is illegal unless permitted by law. Any wager completes the offense.

Illegal gambling operations may come to an officer's attention in many ways (see Fig. 6–12):

Complaint. (Losers often seek revenge.)

Cultivating the gambler who likes to talk. (A police operator may get information and pass it back to a field unit for enforcement or he may participate in the game and signal when the game should be taken.)

Observing that the regular, known gamblers are absent from their hangouts. (The officer may then search and locate their vehicles and, in turn, their game.)

Observing lookouts around places where gambling has been conducted before.

Observing pedestrian traffic or an unusually large number of vehicles around a building that shows no obvious signs of activity.

Being alert when taking reports on other types of crime. (A gambler who loses his paycheck may attempt to report it to the police as a theft or robbery.)

Cards and Dice

In order to effectively enforce violations dealing with cards, the officer should, if he is to testify in court as an expert:

Be able to identify general rules on how the game is played.
  If the officer is unfamiliar with the game, he should have a participant explain details. It is not necessary to identify the game by name.
  If the game is an unusual one, such as Koch, Coon Can, etc., he should make notes on the techniques of play.
Be able to identify the location of each player at a table.
  From a point of observation, make notes, identifying by clothing, hair, and other prominent features those persons who are active players; identify operators of the game if possible.
  Draw a diagram of player location around table for later reference in court if needed.
Wait until betting has gone around the table several times.
Make sure each player has an opportunity to wager a bet.
Establish "thing of value being bet." What is the value of the different colored chips? How much money does each player have in the "kitty"?

Upon entering the game (or if the game is made by an "operator"), the officer should be sure:

There is adequate manpower to properly make the arrests.
All avenues of escape are covered.
Cards, dice and money that are in the middle of the table are seized. Money in front of each player should be noted and returned to owner or booked as evidence. All paraphernalia such as professional-type tables, special doors such as those equipped with a peephole or alarm system, should be taken or photographed as possible evidence.
To search for offensive weapons prior to the conduct of search for evidence.

After arrests are made, the officer should identify the game operators if possible.

Gambling

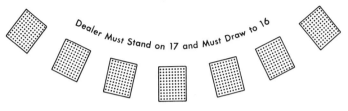

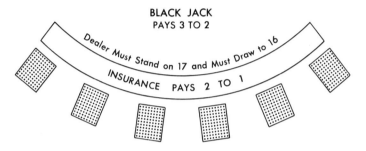

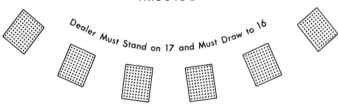

Fig. 6–13. Typical Blackjack layout.

Dice

The techniques of arrest for dice are substantially the same as those for cards. Laws governing dice will vary from state to state. Cite the laws pertaining to your state.

Fig. 6–14. Dice layout found in the more sophisticated gambling operations.

State and Local Laws on Dice. _____

_____

_____

The most common of the dice games is "craps." It is popular since any number of players may participate and the action is fast. Crap games may be played on the street corner or in plush, fully equipped gambling dens. In the more elaborate settings a full layout to assist in the betting may be found. The layout is used almost exclusively for professional games. If the officer is to engage in arrests dealing with commercial gambling activities, he should become familiar with the layout and the terminology used in regard to it (see Fig. 6–13).

The arresting officers of a dice game should check the dice for any evidence of tampering or manipulation. (See Fig. 6–14). If *cheater* dice are used or if there is evidence of an electromagnet being used, it is possible that charges of grand theft or bunco may be pursued.

When gambling evolves from friendly games into com-

Gambling

mercial enterprises, the police are interested in arresting the participants and the operators. If a friendly game becomes a public nuisance, the police will take enforcement action.

Cards and Dice

Sex-Related Offenses

A variety of semi-related crimes are discussed in this chapter. The classifications used do not imply that one type of violation will be associated with another; nor will the offenders have common patterns of operation. Basic classifications are: (1) the sex pervert; (2) the sex degenerate; and (3) other sex offenders, including prostitutes and purveyors of obscenity and pornography.

The Sex Pervert

The category of sex pervert includes those persons who obtain sexual satisfactions in the performance of unnatural sex acts or by unnatural stimulation. Criminal activities engaged in by this type commonly include homosexuality, sodomy, oral copulation, and rape.

In most states these violations, with the exception of rape, are closely related to statutes dealing with homosexuality.

Enforcement of Homosexuality Statutes

This type of criminal enforcement activity causes much concern among personnel about the proper role of police action in this area. It should, however, be emphasized that police involvement is dictated by statute. Therefore, until laws change, the intent of enforcement is not to regulate private or public morals, but to protect society from active, aggressive homosexuals. The police enforcement efforts with regard to these crimes are directed almost exclusively to crimes occurring in public places and to the investigation of complaints.

chapter

7

States vary in identifying specific acts as manifestations of homosexuality. In New York, Penal Law Section 80.1 identifies the crime as sodomy, which includes anal intercourse, "fellatio" (penetration of the mouth by the male sex organ), or "cunnilingus" (the use of the mouth on the female sex organs). Pennsylvania Penal Code Section 501 prohibits carnal knowledge between a human being and an animal, bird, male or female person either by arms or mouth. Florida Statute 800.01 is similar.

These statutes are similar to the laws of other states. Cite below the laws that apply to your own state.

State and Local Statutes. _____

_____

_____

Basically, laws dealing with homosexuality are designed to:

Provide for treatment and rehabilitation for the defendant in a criminal action.

Deter the violator from repeated transgressions.

Deter others from committing the same crime.

Protect society from a potentially dangerous individual.[1]

The law enforcement officer is concerned only with "offenses of homosexuality," not with "homosexuality" as such; thus, the following guidelines are offered not to identify "the homosexual," but only for the purpose of directing officers to those who may commit certain illegal acts.

Some Guidelines for
Recognizing Active Homosexuals

The active, aggressive homosexual can often be recognized because he:

Cruises public places, especially public restrooms, and gives prospects the "eye" (see Figs. 7–1 and 7–2).

[1] Denny F. Pace and Jimmie C. Styles, "The Dynamics of Vice Control" (Unpublished Manuscript, Kent State University, Kent, Ohio, 1969).

The Sex Pervert

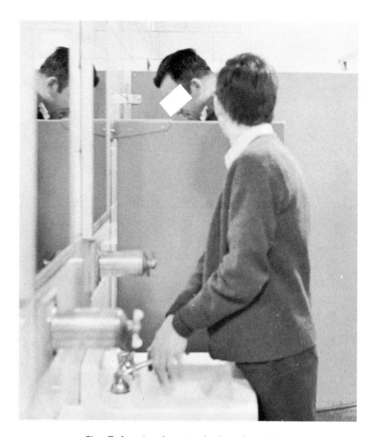

Fig. 7–1. A toilet snipe looking for a date.

Wears extreme clothing styles—e.g., an old man in a purple Nehru suit or a tight-fitting outfit that outlines his private parts. There is a tendency for homosexuals to flaunt their sex publicly.

Uses obnoxious language, including vulgarity and slang terminology relating to other homosexuals.

Openly proclaims he is searching for a model penis.

Has frequent, violent arguments with other homosexuals which result in slapping and scratching each other.

Recognizing female homosexuals is not usually quite as easy. Some of their trademarks might be:

Exaggeration of masculine wear, leather jackets, overcoats, leather boots, no bra, etc.

Sex-Related Offenses

Fig. 7–2. Playing "footsie" in a "tearoom." While this activity is not illegal, it would indicate homosexual activity might follow.

Athletic supporters for underwear; may have artificial penis attached for convenience.

May carry razor, shaving equipment, coke bottles, and penis replacement objects in briefcase.

In applying the term "homosexual," officers should be very cautious since physical features or visible mannerisms do not necessarily identify an individual as a homosexual.

The enforcement officer should direct his efforts toward:

Protecting the citizen from conduct that is offensive in nature as defined by law.

Arresting offenders who are observable to the public or who habituate public parks and restrooms for the purpose of making contacts.

Investigating complaints and taking some positive action when necessary to alleviate a problem situation.

Conducting surveys and studies to determine educational, legislative, and enforcement changes for the alleviation of the sex offender's problem.

Legal statutes and case law will dictate how the law officer conducts an investigation of these violations. In recent

The Sex Pervert

years there has been an unofficial police policy of not operating or otherwise bothering with the investigation of homosexual activity unless there is a complaining party. This policy, while condoning and otherwise offering preferential treatment to the homosexual, eliminates many problems involved in enforcement. Problems frequently encountered in enforcement include:

> The issue of entrapment may arise when the officer becomes an operator. Although most overt homosexuals are quick to approach an operator, it is difficult for a judge and jury to believe such overt activity.
>
> The officer who becomes an operator may establish a set of values in sympathy or antipathy with the homosexual violator. In either situation personal problems may arise.
>
> The very nature of the enforcement of this activity subjects the officer and the department to possible criticism. Courts frequently take exceptions to the role of the vice officer in enforcement matters concerning homosexuals.
>
> The very nature of the enforcement of homosexual violations creates problems of personal safety. Homosexuals are, by nature, often emotionally unstable. Since arrests are frequently made in isolated locations, the arresting officer may expect physical resistance when attempting an arrest.

Techniques for apprehending overt homosexuals are quite simple.

> Merely being "one of the group" is sufficient in places where homosexuals congregate. Aggressive homosexuals will make contact usually quite quickly.
>
> In some areas, cruising the streets slowly will prompt an aggressive homosexual to approach and stop the vehicle.
>
> Observation in public restrooms varies from state to state. Some states sanction fixed observation installations while others have laws closely dictating the types of observations that are legal (see Fig. 7–3). Cite the Law pertaining to your own state.

State and Local Laws Governing Restroom Surveillance.

_____

_____

Sex-Related Offenses

Fig. 7–3. Many public buildings have concealed locations where surveillance may be maintained. Check your state law regarding locations where such techniques may be used.

The following suggestions are offered in regard to legal and moral issues involved in enforcement of laws regarding homosexuals:

Avoid prolonged conversations or observations of homosexual activity. The officer should assume nothing more than the role of a witness.

Good judgment and common sense should dictate the necessity of proper reporting. Officers should choose the most euphemistic phrases and terminology; superfluous wording should be avoided.

The Sex Pervert

Because officers have high ethical and moral standards and are enthusiastic about their profession, it is understandable that they may become too emotionally involved in performing their duties. For this reason, the supervisor must be alert to methods of operating which are so extreme that they may be criticized.

The occasional arrest lost because of the restrictions placed upon operating techniques does not justify the officers' subjecting themselves and their department to questionable, degrading practices.[2]

Rape

This crime denotes an act of sexual intercourse with a female, not the offender's wife, without her voluntary and conscious permission. Proof of elements of rape may be by:

Proof that subject of intercourse is not the wife of the offender. (A husband may be guilty of conspiracy or may be a principal to commit rape on his own wife.)

Proof of penetration, however slight.

Proof that the act was committed without consent. (Degree of resistance necessary may be determined by circumstances. Unsound mind, unconsciousness, or intoxication of the female may show that she was incapable of giving consent.)

Statutory Rape. This is an act of sexual intercourse perpetrated against a female who is under a prescribed age (usually 14 to 18 years). Consent is not a defense. Cite laws pertaining to your own state.

State Laws on Rape. _____

_____

_____

State Law on Statutory Rape. _____

_____

_____

[2]Statements from Captain Harry Nelson, "Vice Management Techniques," A Monograph (Los Angeles: Los Angeles Police Department, 1967).

Sex-Related Offenses

Investigative Techniques. In addition to regular investigative procedures, investigations of such sex crimes usually require that:

A female be present to interview female victims and to take the necessary reports.

The officer be cautious of statements given by young female victims and witnesses. They may swear to a false story in order to save face.

There is a close examination of personal clothing and underclothing of the victim. Rips, semen stains, and hairs may be important evidence.

The Sex Degenerate

This category includes those persons who, by their action patterns, indicate a deviation from the natural act of sexual intercourse. These include: (1) lewd conduct; and (2) child molestation or crimes against children.

Lewd Conduct or Indecent Exposure

Exhibitionism is more frequently committed by men than by women. The victim of the exhibition is usually a girl in her teens. The victim may be selected because of a suspect's fetish—e.g., red dress, glasses, red hair, blonde hair, etc. In many instances the victim is selected as a matter of opportunity or chance (see Figs. 7–4 and 7–5).

Persons involved in this crime are frequently known in the community and will go to any extreme to explain away their behavior. Because of the nature of the crime, the age of the victim, and the community position of the suspect, many cases are settled through medical or psychological referrals.

A statute describing indecent exposure is cited in the New York Penal Code. Section 1140 identifies a violator thus:

Any person who willfully and lewdly exposes his person or the private parts thereof in any public place or in any

The Sex Degenerate

Fig. 7–4. An exhibitionist hanging around the playground.

place where others are present or procures another to so expose himself commits a misdemeanor.

California Penal Code, Section 314.1–2 and Florida Statute 800.03 are similar in content to the New York statute.

Other related sections deal with nudists and outraging public decency. The Michigan Penal Law Manual, Section 125, provides that indecency and immorality, lewd and lascivious cohabitation, gross lewdness, and indecent exposure are misdemeanors. Cite the law pertaining to your own state.

State Law on Lewd Conduct or Indecent Exposure. ____

Officers should be alert to areas where this type of activity is reported. Many cases of this type are cleared by both observing an area and by follow-up investigations of descriptions of vehicles and suspects given by witnesses.

Child Molestation and Related Crimes

These crimes are serious criminal acts and should be so treated. Florida's Child Molester Act, Section 801.02 is

Sex-Related Offenses

Fig. 7–5. Sex fiend? He's not necessarily identifiable by the literature he reads.

typical in its enumeration of acts considered to be child molestation:

> Any offense . . . attempted rape, sodomy, attempted sodomy, crimes against nature, attempted crimes against nature, lewd and lascivious behavior, incest and attempted incest, assault (when a sexual act is completed or attempted) . . . upon a person 14 years of age or under . . .
>
> *The Sex Degenerate*

a.

b.

Fig. 7–6. (a) A majority of child molesters are bold and mobile. (b) Occasionally the molester will be brave enough to operate out of his own house.

The child molester may be identified by his overt actions (see Fig. 7–6). A stranger to the victim will usually:

Sit alone in his automobile on streets where children pass.
Loiter about restrooms or the playground equipment in public parks.
Operate out of his own house and contact the child who passes by.

Sex-Related Offenses

The best method of prevention and apprehension is to have frequent patrols in areas of high crime incidence. The selective use of the Field Interview Card and a close check on employees where children regularly congregate may lessen the chance for repeated crimes of this nature. If the problems persist around parks and public restrooms, increased supervision or closed circuit television usually helps to alleviate them.

About one-half of the crimes of this type are committed by relatives and acquaintances of the victims; in these cases prevention is impossible. When investigating these crimes, the officer should keep both the parents and school officials calm. The victim frequently is not aware of what has happened and may quickly forget the incident if the adults do not panic.

Sex Offender Registration

The enforcement of laws concerning sex offenders may be assisted by statutes requiring certain sex offenders to register when they change address or move from city to city.

The Sex Offender File should include:

Name and current address of known and registered offenders.

Identification of physical traits of active sex offenders.

Methods of operation of offenders, including acts of an unusual nature committed during a crime.

Vehicle identification marks.

The file should be constantly updated with information drawn from the Field Interview Report File. Cite the law that applies to your city and/or state.

State and Local Laws on Sex Offender Registration. ____

_____

_____

Prostitution

If reasonable social control is to be prevalent in a community, a portion of a department's efforts will have to be directed to the enforcement of laws concerning prostitution and related offenses. The permissiveness of a community dictates whether only the most obvious offenders—i.e., the streetwalkers—will be arrested or whether there will also be concentrated efforts against call girls, bar hustlers, and covertly operated houses of prostitution.

The police interest in prostitution is threefold:

To eliminate crimes that are associated with prostitution, such as thefts from person, strong-arm robberies, and traffic in narcotics.

To minimize contact between prostitutes and clients, thus eliminating possible veneral disease contacts.

To keep organized prostitution at a minimum, thus eliminating a highly profitable underworld enterprise, which includes blackmail, extortion, and pimping.

Laws Dealing with Prostitution. There are adequate laws to readily prosecute anyone involved in prostitution or activities related to prostitution.

"The White Slave Traffic Act," Title 18 of the U.S. Code, Sections 2421, 2422, and 2423, prohibits participation in the transportation of a female in interstate or in foreign commerce for the purpose of prostitution, debauchery, or other immoral practices.

Any subterfuge of sending a girl across the state line on a common carrier, etc., does not constitute a defense. Once the intent of the suspects is formulated and a state line is crossed, the violation has been committed.

U.S. Code, Section 2424 deals with the filing of information on alien females with immigration and naturalization agencies. This is done to avoid the importation of females for the purpose of prostitution.

The state laws are diverse, but in general prostitution is prohibited under various rubrics. To engage in prostitution is classed as disorderly conduct in California (Penal Code Section 647b) or as vagrancy in New York (CCP Section 887, 4a-6). It is generally true that the element of *money* be present in addition to the prescribed illegal acts of *lewdness* or *fornication*. Florida Statute 796.07 states that an act of prostitution may be committed without hire.

Other closely related crimes that are violations in most

states are stated below. In each of the following cite the laws that pertain to your own state.

Keeping or residing in house of ill fame (California Penal Code 315). State or local law: _____

_____

Keeping house of ill fame (Florida Statute 796.01). State or local law: _____

_____

Transporting of women for immoral purposes (New York Penal Law 2460.1; Florida Statute 796.07 2d). State or local law: _____

_____

Procuring, inducing, encouraging, coercing, receiving, or giving money for recruiting prostitutes and importing prostitutes into the state (Pennsylvania Penal Code 513 i-iv; Florida Statute 796.03). State or local law: _____

_____

Placing wife in house of prostitution (New York Penal Law 1090). State or local law: _____

_____

Living on proceeds of prostitution (New York Penal Law 1148; Florida Statute 796.05). State or local law: _____

_____

Pimping and pandering (California Penal Code 266h–266i). State or local law: _____

_____

Offering to engage in prostitution (Florida Statute 796.07). State or local law: _____

_____

_____

Prostitution

a. A street hustler looking for a customer.

b. The hustler gets a closer look.

c. The driver doesn't look like a cop, so in she goes.

Fig. 7–7. The street hustler in action.

Forcing one to become a prostitute (Florida Statute 796.04).
State or local law: _____

_____

_____

With minor modifications these crimes are illegal in all states.

Classification of Prostitutes

Prostitutes will vary in their method of operation, depending upon how they were introduced to the business and their physical attractiveness.

The most common type of prostitute to come in contact with law enforcement officers is the *streetwalker* (see Fig. 7–7). She is overt in her operations and takes a chance that the police will not catch her with her "tricks" (customers). Contacts may be made on the street, but cities usually have areas where these violators will congregate. Their presence may be evidenced by the traffic jam that results.

The methods for apprehending a streetwalker may involve visual observation, following her to the location where the sex act is consummated, and making an arrest if all elements required by the state law are present. The transfer of money, if it is an element of the crime, is frequently difficult to prove in these circumstances.

A police operator can sometimes successfully apprehend

Sex-Related Offenses

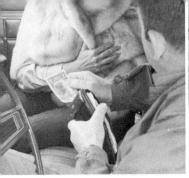

d. The type of "action" dictates the price. Proof of exchange of money may be an element of the crime.

e. The deal is made. The hustler watches for a police tail.

f. Fifteen minutes later the hustler is $20 richer, the trick has peace of mind and no telling what else.

the prostitute either by wearing a disguise and driving a big car or by establishing a method of operating that will cause the prostitute to believe the operator is a bonafide customer. If an operator is contacted by a streetwalker, he should let her take him to her place of business where he may observe:

Persons who are living off the proceeds of the prostitute's earnings.

A hotel or motel that caters to professional prostitutes (Los Angeles City Ordinance prohibits the renting of rooms for the purpose of prostitution, as does the New York Penal Code Multiple Dwelling Law Section 350, 1-D).

Circumstances that would "set-up" the operator as a victim for a strong-arm robbery or a "creep" (a confederate who sneaks into the room of assignation and steals the money and valuables from the "trick's" clothing, which the prostitute has conveniently hung near a door—see Fig. 7–8).

A police operator should be prepared for violence when he must arrest the prostitute, robber, or pimp.

A second type of prostitution is the *call girl*. As one police professor aptly says in his lectures on vice, "The telephone is the call girl's second most important asset." These girls contact "dates" through a "black book" or are referred by other customers or other contact methods centering around the telephone (see Fig. 7–9). When a call girl is discovered, the best way to apprehend her is to get "duked in" as a date by a regular customer.

When a telephone is reportedly being used for call girl

Prostitution

activities, a check should be made on the subscriber and the location. When this is determined, physical surveillance will indicate the amount of action taking place, the identity of the customers, the participating prostitutes, and pimps or madams, if any are present. It is usually not difficult to talk to a customer away from the location and receive information from him that will make it possible for the officer to be referred back to the call girl as a customer. If the police operator is

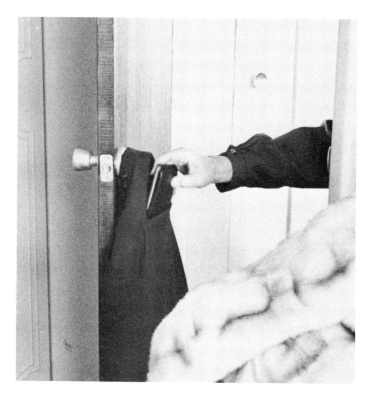

Fig. 7–8. A "creep" appropriating the wallet of a "trick."

to pose as a customer, he should be sure he has the necessary information, such as code words used by referrals from regular customers, in order to be able to convince the prostitute by phone or in person that he is a genuine customer. This information can frequently be obtained from other prostitutes who are anxious to eliminate competition.

Sex-Related Offenses

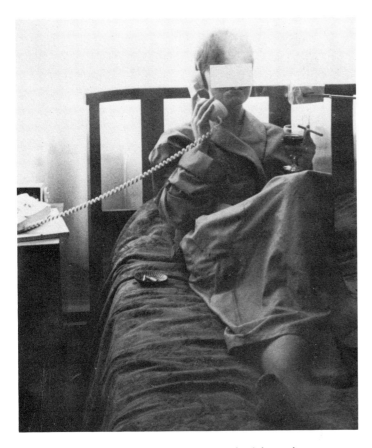

Fig. 7–9. The "call girl" with tools of the trade.

Many call girls operate through answering services or have electronic answering devices on their telephones. When contacting call girls, the police operator should have a confidential phone number in his office available for a return call.

Houses of Prostitution

The prostitute operating out of a house (this may be a hotel or motel room) will usually have someone referring customers to her (see Fig. 7–10). A pimp, a cab driver, or a bartender may be sending customers. Referrals by these procurers are violations (for example, Ohio Revised Statute 2905.18). State and local laws will prompt the vice officer to

Prostitution

Fig. 7–10. A hustler need not be on the street.

develop enforcement techniques to secure convictions on these subjects. Cite the laws that pertain to your city and/or state.

State and Local Laws on Procuring and Pandering. ____

When possible, raids on regularly established houses should be based upon a search warrant or warrant of arrest for the house operators. If a location becomes a public nuisance or is continually a disorderly house, abatement proceedings should be initiated to close the house completely. In most states, abatement may be brought against any public nuisance. In order to substantiate abatement proceedings, the following procedures should be used.

Sex-Related Offenses

The person in charge of a public dwelling where an arrest for prostitution has been made shall be:

Shown the person arrested.

Informed of the arrest and any statements made by the arrested persons as to the use of the premises for prostitution.[3]

The arrest report should include:

The name, address, and the capacity of the person so informed.

His statements and reaction when informed that prostitution was being practiced on the premises.

All obvious, open, and flagrant violations involving lewd conduct should be cited.

The following suggestions give general procedures to be used in apprehending the prostitute:

In prostitution offenses, it is desired that the police officer not lend himself to the character of an aggressive "trick."

The operator does not suggest to the prostitute the type of sex desired.

The operator should not give the prostitute the opportunity to evoke, as a defense in court, testimony that the operator solicited her.

Probably the best operating technique is to play the shy "trick" and thus provide the opportunity for eliciting conversation from the prostitute.[4]

There are as many methods of operation for the prostitute as there are prostitutes. Most prostitutes are not very difficult to arrest once they come to the attention of the police.

[3]*Ibid.* This applies only in areas where there are statutes prohibiting such violations as keeping a house of prostitution, operating a disorderly house, or a house of assignation.

[4]*Ibid.*

Prostitution

If officers have good sources of information, overt prostitution can be reasonably controlled.

The uniformed officer, although not assigned exclusively to vice, should not overlook violations of prostitution. This is especially important for abatement proceedings. While it may not be feasible for patrol officers to physically arrest prostitutes in the overt act, the patrol officer may utilize vagrancy and loitering laws for preventive enforcement. All patrol officers should be required by departmental regulations to report all observed violations in writing.

The prostitute employs a number of subterfuges for her activities that frequently make operating and arrests difficult. For example, an answering service will make it difficult to arrest the prostitute unless the officer is able to maintain informant contacts. The "lonely hearts club" activity will necessitate slow, cautious operation to separate the legitimate "lonely hearts" from the professional prostitutes. The female who uses the computer to select a mate is beyond the apprehension capabilities of most local agencies. The same is true of the "secretarial services," the "professional party girls," the "occasional party girls," and the occasional prostitutes. In most instances, the latter categories do not present an overt problem. These violators are usually not encountered except upon complaint.

Each officer will tend to establish techniques that are most compatible with his individual capabilities in effecting the arrest.

Obscenity and Pornography

The police enforcement of laws dealing with areas of obscenity and pornography have been clouded because of the lack of consistency on the part of the courts. Local courts feel it is their duty to establish community behavior standards while the Supreme Court has ruled that materials of this nature are not entitled to constitutional protection offered the normally spoken and published communication.[5] Until these

[5]Pace and Styles, op. cit., a section of which is devoted to the discussion of the absolutist position held by several members of the Supreme Court.

Sex-Related Offenses

problems are resolved, the police are still faced with a large number of local laws upon which they are commanded to act.

Definition of Obscenity

A thing, as applied to contemporary community standards, is obscene if:

The material is patently offensive.

Considered as a whole, the dominant theme or purpose is an appeal to prurient interests.

It is utterly without redeeming social importance.

The character of the material or the circumstances of its dissemination is to be considered in judging if a matter is obscene.

Pornography is writings, pictures, etc., that are intended to arouse sexual desires. Each state has its own coded definition of material generally acceptable to the community at large.

Obscenity Laws. Federal statutes are comprehensive with respect to obscenity violations. Title 18 U.S. Code, Sections 1461 through 1465, covers the following violations:

Section 1461: Mailing obscene or crime inciting matter. This section includes any publication of an indecent nature and any item for preventing conception or inducing abortion. (This is supplemented by Title 39 U.S. Code, Section 4001 or 4006.)

Section 1462: Importing or transporting obscene matters.

Section 1464: Broadcasting obscene matter.

Section 1465: Transporting obscene matter for sale or distribution.

Obscenity Laws of New York. Penal Law Section 43 (outraging public decency) covers *any act* not otherwise specifically enumerated as a crime which in fact openly outrages public decency.

Penal Law Section 1140a subsections 1–4 (shows and exhibits) prohibits preparing, advertising, giving, directing, or participating in any obscene, indecent or immoral event.

Obscenity and Pornography

Penal Law 1141–1 covers obscene prints and articles. Other sections cover signs, billboards, sales, abortifacients, etc.[6] Pornography is restricted from sale to minors under eighteen years of age.

The Pennsylvania Penal Code 524 and Florida Statute 847.011 prohibit similar activities relating to obscenity and pornography. Cite the laws that pertain to your state.

State and Local Obscenity Laws. _____

_____

_____

General Police Policy

While the laws are specific on obscenity violations, there are broad standards as to what constitutes obscene matter. The police should attempt to avoid the role of community censors.

Much criticism has been directed toward police vice details for their activities in this field of enforcement. While departments may legally enforce obscenity statutes, the question of *what is obscene* still must be clarified by the courts.

There are a number of alternatives to physical arrests in obscenity cases. These alternatives may be effective in curbing the distribution of obscene material.

Action "in rem": an action against the material itself which provides for seizure by court order. This takes the police out of the censor's role in determining what is obscene.[7]

Injunction against known purveyors of obscene materials. This places the court in the position of having to make the decisions regarding the question of obscenity.

An alternative to direct physical arrest is the indirect method of filing a complaint or securing an indictment.

These procedures are offered not to discourage police arrest action, but to properly place the responsibility for judgment of materials that are questionable in the hands of the court.

[6]This section will probably be modified due to the recent changes in New York abortion statutes.

[7]Florida Statute 847.03 provides that an officer may seize obscene material. This places the police in the position of being censors.

Sex-Related Offenses

Obscene Phone Calls

Police complaint desks are frequently notified by female victims of obscene telephone calls. The victim should be advised to:

Hang up immediately after discovering that a call is obscene.

Not to give information on the phone unless the caller's identity is known.

Contact the telephone company for assistance—i.e., new number or trace—if calls persist.

Enforcement has been strengthened by a federal statute that prohibits obscene telephone calls.

State laws and local ordinances, in essence, are similar to Pennsylvania Penal Code Section 414.1. A person is guilty of an offense who:

Telephones another person and addresses to or about such other person any lewd, lascivious, or indecent words or language; or

Anonymously telephones another person repeatedly for the purpose of annoying, molesting, or harassing such other person or his or her family.

Because of the difficulty of identifying offending callers, the enforcement of this statute has been limited.

Two new developments will facilitate the detection and prosecution of offending telephone callers:

Telephone companies are developing a system that will automatically identify the instrument from which a telephone call is being made.[8] This system has the unique feature of keeping the line open until the person being called hangs up.

The voice print or speech spectrogram may be used for the purpose of identifying the caller.

Some important ideas and problems related to the field of vice law enforcement have been ignored or omitted from this book. In most instances, these omissions have been intentional. There has been an attempt to stress the important and most widely used laws dealing with each type of violation. Obviously, not all problems associated with a specific violation are resolved. Many social problems are left to the logic and good judgment of the police investigator.

[8]A dial pulse indicator allows a trace to be made. There do not have to be any words spoken.

Obscenity and Pornography

Suggested References

AMERICAN ACADEMY OF POLITICAL AND SOCIAL SCIENCE. "An Interdisciplinary Attack on Organized Crime," *The Annals*, May 1969.

CRESSEY, DONALD R. *Theft of the Nation*. New York: Harper & Row, Publishers, 1969.

DRZAZGA, JOHN. *Wheels of Fortune*. Springfield, Ill.: Charles C Thomas, 1951.

EARHART, LT. ROBERT. "Intelligence Gathering, Evaluation, Dissemination and Surveillance." Monograph. Department of State Police, Lansing, Michigan, 1969.

EGEN, FREDERICK W. *Plainclothesman*. New York: Arco Publishing Company, Inc., 1963.

KING, RUFUS. *Gambling and Organized Crime*. Washington, D.C.: Public Affairs Press, 1969.

MCDONNELL, RICHARD E. "Police Management Applications." Poughkeepsie, New York: I.B.M. Customer Executive Program, April 1968.

NELSON, CAPT. HARRY. "Vice Management Techniques." Monograph. Los Angeles Police Department, Los Angeles, 1967.

NEW YORK STATE. *Combatting Organized Crime*. 1965 Oyster Bay Conference. Albany, N.Y.: The Governor's Office, 1966.

PACE, DENNY F., and JIMMIE C. STYLES. "The Dynamics of Vice Control." Unpublished manuscript, Kent State University, Kent, Ohio, 1969.

PETERSON, VIRGIL W. *Gambling: Should It Be Legalized?* Springfield, Ill.: Charles C Thomas, 1951.

PRESIDENT'S COMMISSION ON LAW ENFORCEMENT AND ADMINISTRATION OF JUSTICE. *Task Force Report: Organized Crime*. Washington, D.C.: Govenment Printing Office, 1967.

SALERNO, RALPH, and JOHN S. TOMPKINS. *The Crime Con-*

federation. Garden City, N.Y.: Doubleday and Company, Inc., 1969.

SCHWARTZ, MURRAY R. "The Lawyer's Professional Responsibility and Interstate Organized Crime," *The Notre Dame Lawyer*, XXXVIII (1963), 711–26.

SKOLNICK, JEROME H. *Justice Without Trial.* New York: John Wiley & Sons, Inc., 1966.

STOKES, HAROLD R. *Vice Enforcement and Its Dynamic Relationship in the Administration of Criminal Justice.* Published doctoral dissertation. Los Angeles: University of Southern California, 1965.

WILLIAMS, JOHN B. *Vice.* Walteria, Calif.: Walteria California Research Associates, 1964.

Appendix I: Cue Sheets

TM-(L)-2506/000/01

EVENT REPORT CUE SHEET[1]

Item 1. Event Report
_____
         (Type of Report)

Reporting Officer:
Item 2. _____ / _____ / _____
         (Name)   (Serial Number) (Division of Assignment)

Item 3.
_____
         (Type(s) of Crime: Insert from list of crime classifications:
         Indicate attempt or conspiracy to commit. If more than one
         crime involved repeat "Item 3," followed by the additional
         classification for each crime.)

Date and Time Reported:
Item 4.
_____
         Month/Day/Year   Example: 12/6/66.
         (Use 24-hour designation. Example: 1315)

Location of Occurrence:
Item 5.
_____
         (Type of Premises)

Item 6.
_____
         (Address: Number   Street   City)

Time of Occurrence:
Item 7.
_____
         Month/Day/Year   Hour/Minutes (Use 24-hour clock)

Item 8. People (Use People Cue Sheet[s])
Item 9.
_____
         (Approving Authority: Inserted by Reviewer)

Item 10.
_____
         (Clearance: By Arrest, Other (State), Unfounded)

Item 11.
_____
                    (Property Description)

Item 12.
_____
         (Event Number: Blank if new report; if follow-up information,
         insert number of original report.)

Item 13. (Narrative)

[1] This form and the two following are taken as samples from the Los Angeles Police Department, Phase I. Operating System Description, Technical Memorandum TM (L) 2506/000/01. (Santa Monica, Calif.: Systems Development Corp., 1965), pp. 77–81. These examples are cited only as theoretical models and do not imply that they will be adopted by any department for official use.

PEOPLE CUE SHEET

Item 8. _____ / _____ / _____
      (Name: Last name first)   (Role)   (Crime)

Descriptors

A. _____
   (Sex/Descent)

B. ____ / ____ / _____
   (Birth date)

C. _____
   (Place of Birth)

D. _____ / _____
   (Height/Weight)

E. _____
   (Hair)

F. _____
   (Eyes)

G. _____
   (Complexion)

H. _____
   (Residence address)

J. _____
   (Residence telephone)

K. _____
   (Occupation)

L. _____
   (Address of employment)

M. _____
   (Telephone number of employment)

N. _____
   (If suspect arrested, booking number)

P. _____
   (Nickname or alias)

R. _____
   (Driver's license number)

S. _____
   (Social Security number)

T. _____
   (Vehicle description)
1. _____
   (Year/Make)
2. _____
   (Body style)
3. _____
   (Color)
4. _____
   (License number (state, year))
5. _____
   (Other identifying features)

U. _____
   (Clothing)

W. _____
   (Other identifying characteristics)

X. _____
   (Other suspect information)

(Items A through M relate to all roles; items N through X relate only to suspect.)

BOOKING REPORT CUE SHEET

Item 1.   Booking Report
_____
          (Type of Report)

Reporting Officer:
Item 2.   /   /
_____
          (Name)   (Serial Number)   (Division of Assignment)

Location of Occurrence:
Item 3.
_____
          (Location of booking)

Time of Occurrence:
Item 4.   /
_____
          (Month/Day/Year)   (Hour/Minutes)

Police Department Booking Number:
Item 5.   (Automatically Assigned)
_____

County Booking Number:
Item 6.
_____
          (Insert if known)

Charge(s):
Item 7.
_____
          (If warrant, insert number; include type of charge: Misdemeanor,
          felony, other.)

Identifiable Personal Property:
Item 8.
_____

People:
Item 9.   (Use People Cue Sheet[s])

Other information on the booking report which may be retained
in the System:

    Emergency notification information

    Vehicle impound information

    Evidence booked information

    Special medical problems information

    Amount of money in prisoner's personal property

    Other articles of personal property

    Probable investigative unit (probably will not be determined
       by reporting officer)

    Location crime committed and date, time arrested, and
       arresting officers (better input from event or arrest report)

    Name of searching officer

    Name of booking officer

Appendix I: Cue Sheets

This information was taken from Crime Commission Reports, the Omnibus Crime Bill and Safe Streets Act of 1968, and (S-30) the Organized Crime Bill of 1969.

1. An increase in the efficiency of the evidence-gathering process (e.g., electronic surveillance for limited crimes by court order).

2. Specifically constituted, long tenured grand juries to replace the present system.

3. Improved witness immunity laws; establishment of residential communities for some witnesses who need continued protection.

4. Improved perjury laws in eliminating two-witness and direct evidence rules.

5. Centralized data-processing system for organized crime intelligence.

6. Evidence suppressed by suspected corrupt court action would be subject to appeal.

7. Persons engaged in continuing illegal business, in a management position, will be subject to increased penalties.

8. A prohibition of illegally gained funds being invested in a legitimate business.

9. Bribery and corruption of local officials or police made a federal crime.

10. A gambling operation from which five or more persons derive income and which has been in operation more than thirty days or exceeds $2,000 daily income would become a federal crime.

11. Each state, under the U.S. Attorney General, would form special units to serve as liaison with specialized units at the local level, who in turn would be charged with the establishing of procedures and the gathering of evidence for prosecutions.

12. Federal support to regional intelligence gathering, study of organized crime, and dissemination of information back to local agencies.

13. The Organized Crime and Racketeering Section to conduct training for local law enforcement officers.

14. Public and private crime investigating commissions be organized and maintained on a full-time basis.

15. Federal and state regulatory agencies and private business associations to develop strategies for uncovering organized crime tactics.

16. News media encouraged to write exposés informing the public of corrupt conditions in the community.

Appendix II: Future Efforts to Control Organized Crime